Time for Italian

All it takes is twenty minutes a day

Donatella de Ferra
Marina Mozzon-McPherson

Stanley Thornes (Publishers) Ltd

First published in 1999 by:
Stanley Thornes (Publishers) Ltd
Ellenborough House
Wellington Street
CHELTENHAM GL50 1YW
England

A catalogue record for this book is available
from the British Library

99 00 01 02 03 / 10 9 8 7 6 5 4 3 2 1

ISBN 0-7487-3881-9 (book)
ISBN 0-7487-3883-5 (complete pack)
ISBN 0-7487-3882-7 (cassettes)

Also available in the *Time for Languages* series:

Time for French, Paul Durrant
Time for German, Corinna Schicker
Time for Portuguese, Sue Tyson-Ward
Time for Spanish, Robert Clarke

Cover: Joanna Kerr

Typeset by Action Publishing Technology Limited, Gloucester
Recorded at the Speech Recording Studio, London
Voice artists: Anna Maria Rubino, Michela Ravano, Aldo Alessio
Printed and bound in Great Britain by T. J. International Ltd, Padstow, Cornwall

How to make the best use of *Time for Italian*

The material in *Time for Italian* has been designed for you to complete one unit every day, but you are in control. If you want to cover several units in a day, then do that. Do try, however, to stick to a sensible routine so that you cover a number of units spread over the course of one week, rather than ten sessions at the week-end. You will retain so much more if you 'drip-feed' yourself. You should ideally work through the units in sequence, but again, you are in control. Choose a method which suits you best.

Start by listening to the **Vocabolario** (vocabulary) section on the recording and follow the words in your book. Listen carefully to the pronunciation and try to mimic it as best you can. There is space on the recording for you to repeat the word imme-diately after the actor. If possible, practise out loud, and don't be shy! The more you get used to hearing your own voice speaking Italian, the easier it will become. The vocabulary is read out on the cassette until Unit 27. In the later units you can still practise reading the words and phrases out loud; you can check your pronunciation when you listen to the dialogues.

Now listen to the **Dialoghi** (dialogues) section, first of all without following the transcript in the book, and then using the text. This uses the words you have been practising already. See how much you can understand before you consult the text. Don't worry if there are parts you miss – just try to catch the drift of what is said.

Once you have read through the text and unravelled its contents you are ready for the **Esercizi** (exercises). Some of these involve the recording, some don't. In Exercise 3 of some units you will be asked to take part in a speaking activity. Usually this takes the form of a dialogue with an actor on the recording. You will be given prompts in English on the recording, written in the book or by means of pic-tures. Make sure you follow the sequence of these prompts carefully to guide you in your responses. You will soon get used to the method used here, and you will find it invaluable in gaining confidence in speaking naturally.

Finally read the **Tip** (usually a grammar hint) and **Panorama italiano**, which gives you some background on the culture and lifestyle of Italian-speaking Europe.

Do come back to units in the future to refresh your memory. Once you have covered the unit with the help of the book, you will find that playing the recordings in your car or while ironing, or whatever, will prove invaluable.

Good luck and enjoy learning Italian!

Contents

Greetings

Saying hello

Vocabolario (Basic vocabulary)

ciao	hello/goodbye (*informal*)
buongiorno	good morning
buona sera	good afternoon, good evening
buona notte	good night
signor + name	Mr + name
signora + name	Mrs + name, Ms + name
signorina + name	Miss + name
dottor + name	Doctor + name
ingegner + name	Engineer + name
professor + name	Professor + name

Dialoghi (Dialogues)

Mr Bianco and Mrs Barilla meet in the morning at the coffee bar.

Signor Bianco	Buongiorno, signora Barilla.
Signora Barilla	Buongiorno, signor Bianco.

Mr Manin and Miss Sgorlon leave the office at 5.00 p.m. Mr Manin has a degree in engineering.

Signorina Sgorlon	Buona sera, ingegner Manin.
Ingegner Manin	Buona sera, signorina Sgorlon.

Roberta Verdi leaves her friend Franco's house at night after a party.

Roberta	Buona notte, Franco.
Franco	Buona notte.

Esercizi (Exercises)

1 Reorder the pictures. Listen to the recording and list the greetings in the order in which you hear them. (*Answers on page 126.*)

A _____   B _____   C _____   D _____

2 Stretch yourself. Complete this puzzle in Italian. In the shaded column you will find another way to say 'Hello!' (*Answers on page 126.*)

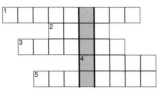

Clues **1** Good evening **2** Hello! **3** Miss … in the second dialogue **4** Roberta's surname in the third dialogue **5** a person with a degree in engineering

3 Let's greet each other. Listen to the recording and give the appropriate Italian greetings. Follow the prompts below and on the recording. You speak first. (*Answers on page 126.*)

1. Say 'Good morning, Signora Barilla.'
2. Greet a friend.
3. Say good evening to Mr Manin. (Remember he has a degree in engineering.)
4. Say good night to Marta.

Tip

Note the loss of the final **-e** when the titles **dottore, professore, ingegnere** and **signore** are followed by a person's name:

Buongiorno, dottore	*but*	**Buongiorno, dottor Accinelli**
Buongiorno, signore	*but*	**Buongiorno, signor Cattaneo**

Now complete the next two examples by yourself. (*Answers on page 126.*)

Buona sera, ingegnere	*but*	**Buona sera, ... De Benedetti**
Buona notte, professore	*but*	**Buona notte, ... Prodi**

Panorama italiano

Titles and social status
In Italy the use of titles is widespread. Everybody who has completed a degree is addressed as **dottore**. **Professore** and **ingegnere** are also used as titles. **Signora** covers both Mrs and Ms, while **Signorina** is used only for a very young woman.

Greetings

Saying who you are/what you're called

Vocabolario (Basic vocabulary)

piacere	how do you do?, pleased to meet you
molto lieto	how do you do? (*when a man replies*)
molto lieta	how do you do? (*when a woman replies*)
scusi	excuse me
come si chiama?	what is your name? (*formal*)
mi chiamo Roberta Verdi	my name is Roberta Verdi
per favore	please
grazie	thank you
prego	don't mention it
lentamente	slowly

Dialoghi (Dialogues)

Mr Cattaneo and Miss Sgorlon meet for the first time.

Signorina Sgorlon	Scusi, come si chiama?
Signor Cattaneo	Mi chiamo Carlo Cattaneo.
Signorina Sgorlon	Piacere. Maria Sgorlon.
Signor Cattaneo	Molto lieto.

At the hotel, Mr Cattaneo is asked for his name by the receptionist.

Receptionist	Buona sera. Come si chiama?
Signor Cattaneo	Buona sera, mi chiamo Carlo Cattaneo.
Receptionist	Lentamente, per favore.
Signor Cattaneo	CARLO CATTANEO.
Receptionist	Grazie.
Signor Cattaneo	Prego.

Mr Cattaneo introduces himself to Mrs Malagodi.

Signor Cattaneo	Buongiorno, mi chiamo Carlo Cattaneo.
Signora Malagodi	Molto lieta. Mi chiamo Federica Malagodi.
Signor Cattaneo	Piacere.

Esercizi (Exercises)

1   Broken dialogues. Listen to the two dialogues on the recording and fill in the missing words. (*Answers on page 126.*)

   1. .... Marta Marzotto.

      ...., mi chiamo Felice Cavenago.

   2. Ciao, mi chiamo ....

      Ciao, ... Giulia.

2 The odd-one-out. Circle the word/expression that does not belong to the group. (*Answers on page 126.*)

1	molto lieto	piacere	ciao
2	mi chiamo	piacere	scusi
3	grazie	lentamente	prego

3 Let's introduce ourselves. Complete the dialogue following the prompts below and on the recording. (*Answers on page 126.*)

  1. Say good morning.
  2. Ask him to say it again slowly, please.
  3. Now reply 'How do you do?' and add your name.

Tip

Compare the sounds **c** for **ciao** (English sound of **ch**ur**ch**) and **c** for **come** (English sound of **c**at).

Listen to the dialogues and the recording for Esercizio 1 again and notice the difference between the way the following sounds have been pronounced: **piacere**; **Federica, come**; **Felice, ciao**; **mi chiamo**. Place the words in the appropriate column. (*Answers on page 126.*)

c like **church**	c like **cat**
1	4
2	5
3	6

Panorama italiano

Italian names
Most male names end in **-o** (Carlo, Roberto, etc.) while the names of women usually end in **-a** (Roberta, Federica, Marta, etc.).

Do you already know any Italian names of men or women? Do they conform to this pattern?

Ring **M** or **F** to indicate whether the following first names are male or female. (*Answers on page 126.*)

Francesca M F   Marta M F   Marco M F   Carlo M F

3 Greetings

Saying where you come from

Vocabolario (Basic vocabulary)

sì	yes
no	no
sono (essere)	I am
è?	are you? (*formal*)
e	and
e Lei?	and you? (*formal*)
di	from
Roma	Rome
inglese	English
italiano, italiana	Italian
americano, americana	American

The Italian forms given in brackets are those you would look up in a dictionary
(**essere** 'to be').

Dialoghi (Dialogues)

Mr Cattaneo is on holiday at Punta Ala, in southern Tuscany, and is getting acquainted with a neighbour on the beach.

Signor Cattaneo	Buongiorno. Sono Carlo Cattaneo.
Neighbour	Piacere. Jane Murphy.
Signor Cattaneo	Piacere. È inglese?
Neighbour	Sì, sono inglese. Sono di Bath, e Lei?
Signor Cattaneo	Sono italiano, sono di Roma.

Mr Roberto Costa from Milan introduces himself.

Roberto Costa	Buongiorno, sono Roberto Costa. Sono italiano. Sono di Milano.

Madonna from New York introduces herself.

Madonna	Buongiorno, sono Madonna. Sono americana. Sono di New York.

Esercizi (Exercises)

1 Listen to the two dialogues and complete the grid in English. (*Answers on page 126.*)

	1	2
name		
nationality		
town		

2 Match the two halves of the sentences. (*Answers on page 126.*)

A Sono di	**1** inglese.
B Mi chiamo	**2** Roma.
C Sono	**3** molto lieto.
D Piacere, ...	**4** Marco.

3 Label the pictures with the appropriate nationality. (*Answers on page 126.*)

1   **2**   **3**

A americana   **B** italiano   **C** inglese

4 The interview. Listen to the dialogue and reply to the questions by following the prompts below and on the recording. (*Answers on page 126.*)

1. Say your name. **2.** Say 'Yes, I am English'. **3.** Say where you are from.
4. Say 'don't mention it'.

Tip

In Italian 'I am' is **sono** and the polite form for 'you are' or 'are you' is **è** or **è?**
The word **Lei** is the polite form for 'you'. It is used to address somebody, male or female, who you don't know at all, you don't know very well or you feel you owe respect to (e.g. your boss, an elderly person, etc.)

Note also that a woman will refer to herself as **italiana, americana**, while a man will say **italiano, americano**. Nationalities which end in **-e** are the same for both men and women: **John è inglese, Sarah è inglese.**

When **e** comes before a noun starting with a vowel, it can change into **ed**, e.g. **Roberto ed Antonio**.

Panorama italiano

Campanilismo
For historical reasons Italians are very attached to the particular areas they come from – their region, town or village. They will describe themselves as **toscano** if they come from Tuscany but tend to stress the city as well as the region (e.g. **fiorentino** if they come from Florence, **romano** if they come from Rome; **milanese** if they are from Milan).

The strong attachment to the place of origin, accompanied by the feeling of superiority it engenders, is known as '**campanilismo**' from the word '**campanile**' (bell tower).

It would be a good idea to familiarize yourself with a map of Italy. Do you know where some of the main cities are: Milan, Turin, Venice, Florence, Rome, Naples? (*Answers on page 126.*)

UNIT 4 Greetings

Asking people about their jobs

Vocabolario (Basic vocabulary)

scozzese	Scottish
qui	here
in vacanza	on holiday
anche	also
per lavoro	for work
che lavoro fa?	what is your job?
io	I
medico	doctor (m, *used for men and women*)
operaio	factory worker (m)
operaia	factory worker (f)
calciatore	football player
insegnante	teacher (m and f)
insegnante di italiano	teacher of Italian

Dialoghi (Dialogues)

Dr Laura Ferrari meets a British tourist in Jesolo, near Venice.

Dott. Ferrari	Buongiorno, sono Laura Ferrari.
Paul McPherson	Piacere, Paul McPherson.
Dott. Ferrari	Scusi, Lei è inglese?
Paul McPherson	No, sono scozzese, di Edimburgo.
Dott. Ferrari	È qui in vacanza?
Paul McPherson	Sono qui in vacanza e anche per lavoro. Sono insegnante di italiano. E Lei è in vacanza?
Dott. Ferrari	No, io sono di Jesolo. Sono medico.

Six people are stranded in an airport lounge. They introduce themselves and describe their jobs.

Sono Roberto Baggio, sono calciatore. E Lei che lavoro fa?

Sono Tiziana Frausin, sono insegnante. E Lei che lavoro fa?

Sono Pia Pupini, anche io sono insegnante. E Lei che lavoro fa?

Sono Sergio Frausin, sono medico. E Lei che lavoro fa?

Sono Renata Gasperini, sono operaia. E Lei che lavoro fa?

Sono Franco Pupini, anche io sono operaio.

Tip

To help you remember the masculine and feminine forms of names of jobs in Italian, associate them with the names of two famous people (one male, one female) or two people you know.

Esercizi (Exercises)

1   The workplace. Listen to both recordings again and match each speaker with the correct workplace. (*Answers on page 126.*)

A ....   B ....   C ....   D ....
   ....
   ....

2   Your job. Look up the Italian word for your job in the dictionary, then complete the sentences below.

Sono .... (your name).
Sono .... (your job).

3   Other people's jobs. Intonation practice. Remember that when you are speaking the only way you can show you are asking a question is to let your voice rise at the end of a sentence. Listen to six people and follow the prompts below and on the recording. (*Answers on page 126.*)

1. • Ask 'Are you a teacher?' • Say your name, and then your job.
2. • Ask 'Are you a football player?' • Say your name, and then your job.
3. • Ask 'Are you a doctor?' • Say your name, and then your job.
4. • Ask 'Are you a factory worker (m)?' • Say your name, and then your job.
5. • Ask 'Are you a factory worker (f)?' • Say your name, and then your job.
6. • Ask 'Are you a teacher?'

Tip

In Italian you do not normally use subject pronouns (the words for 'I', 'you', etc.), unless you want to give emphasis: **Io sono Pia** *I* am Pia.

Nouns refer to people, animals, things or ideas. Italian nouns have a gender: they are either masculine or feminine. Their endings can give you a clue as to the gender. The most common ending for masculine nouns is **-o**; giorn**o**, lavor**o**, while for feminine nouns it is **-a**: signor**a**, vacan**za**. The ending **-e** can appear on both masculine and feminine nouns: signor**e** (m), nott**e** (f). Some occupations have two separate endings, **-o** for a man and **-a** for a woman: operai**o**/operai**a**; while others have the same ending, often **-e** for both: insegnant**e** (m and f).

Panorama italiano

Women and family names
Italian women do not lose their maiden name on getting married but add their husband's name to their maiden name. Official communications will always bear their maiden name. This accounts for all the double-barrelled names found on Italian doorbells.

Women and professions
Contemporary Italian uses the masculine form to designate some professions for women: **medico, ingegnere, professore.**

Greetings

Saying where you work

Vocabolario (Basic vocabulary)

ecco	here/there is
come va?	how are you? (*informal*)
un, un', una, uno	a, an
uno studente	a student (m)
una studentessa	a student (f)
una segretaria	a secretary (f)
un segretario	a secretary (m)
lavoro (lavorare)	I work
studio (studiare)	I study
in	in
una ditta	a firm
un'amica	a friend (f)
un amico	a friend (m)
Venezia	Venice
una commessa	a saleswoman, shop assistant (f)
un commesso	a salesman, shop assistant (m)
un grande magazzino	a department store
una scuola	a school
di	of

Dialoghi (Dialogues)

Valentina and Emanuela go to a cafe. Valentina spots her friend Fulvio and they join him.

Valentina	Ecco Fulvio. Ciao Fulvio.
Fulvio	Ciao Valentina, come va?
Valentina	Emanuela è un'amica di Venezia.
Fulvio	Piacere, è studentessa anche Lei?
Emanuela	No, io sono segretaria. Lavoro in una ditta.

Barbara and Byrom have just met at a party.

Barbara	Piacere, Barbara.
Byrom	Piacere, Byrom.
Barbara	Scusi, come si chiama? Lentamente prego.
Byrom	BY-ROM, è un nome americano. Sono di Bangor nel Maine.
Barbara	È studente?
Byrom	Nel Maine sono studente, studio italiano. Qui sono insegnante in una scuola di inglese. E Lei?
Barbara	Io sono commessa. Lavoro in un grande magazzino ... *and ... I study English at night classes.*

Esercizi (Exercises)

1   True or false? Listen to the two dialogues again and tick the correct box. (*Answers on page 126.*)

		T	F
A	Three of the five speakers are women.	☐	☐
B	Emanuela is a student.	☐	☐
C	Barbara is a salesperson.	☐	☐
D	Emanuela comes from Venice.	☐	☐
E	Byrom is Scottish.	☐	☐

2   Who does what? Listen to the recording and reply to the questions. Follow the prompts below and on the recording. (*Answers on page 126.*)

1. Say 'No, he is a student'. **2.** Say 'No, she is a student'.   **3.** Say, 'No, I am a teacher, Laura is a doctor'.   **4.** Say, 'No, she is a secretary in a firm.'

3   Put a tick to show where you are most likely to find these people. (*Answers on page 126.*)

	in una scuola	in una ditta	in un grande magazzino
A un'insegnante			
B un insegnante			
C una commessa			
D una segretaria			
E uno studente			
F una studentessa			
G un commesso			

Tip

è means 'he/she/it is' as well as 'you are' (polite form).

The word for 'a, an' can have four different forms in Italian, depending on the gender and the initial letter(s) of the word that follows.
Before feminine nouns it is **una**, but **un'** if the noun starts with a vowel (**a-/e-/i-/o-/u-**):

una commessa, una segretaria, un'amica.

Before masculine nouns it is **un**, but **uno** if the noun starts with **z-** or **s-** + consonant (a consonant is any letter except a/e/i/o/u):

un calciatore, un amico, uno studente, uno zio.

You do not need the article in Italian when you say what someone's job is:

| John is a student. | *but* | **Fulvio è studente.** |
| I am a secretary. | *but* | **Io sono segretaria.** |

Panorama italiano

Studying foreign languages is very popular in Italy and many Italians attend classes at private institutions, which can be quite expensive. English is especially popular.

6 People

Talking about one's family

Vocabolario

ma	but
questo, questa	this
mio figlio	my son
mia figlia	my daughter
mio marito	my husband
mia madre	my mother
suo padre	his/her father
sua moglie	his wife
suo fratello	his/her brother
sua sorella	his/her sister

Dialogo

Mr and Mrs Gandolfi meet Mrs Bartoli and they introduce their families.

Signora Gandolfi	Buongiorno, signora Bartoli.
Signora Bartoli	Buongiorno, signora Gandolfi. Questo è mio figlio Giorgio e questa è sua sorella Mariella.
Signora Gandolfi	Ciao Giorgio, ciao Mariella. Questo è Valerio, mio marito.
Signora Bartoli	Molto lieta.
Signor Gandolfi	Piacere. Questa è mia figlia Valentina.
Signora Bartoli	Ciao Valentina.
Signor Gandolfi	È qui a Porto Rotondo in vacanza?
Signora Bartoli	No, mio marito è qui per lavoro. E Lei è qui in vacanza?
Signor Gandolfi	Sì, io sono qui in vacanza ma mia madre è di Porto Rotondo.

Esercizi

1 Comprehension. Listen to the dialogue again and answer the following questions in English. (*Answers on page 126.*)

   A How many children does Mrs Gandolfi have? ....

   B Who comes from Porto Rotondo? ....

   C Who works in Porto Rotondo? ....

   D What is the name of Giorgio's sister? ....

2 Family tree. Look at how Mrs Gandolfi introduces members of her family. Then complete the empty frames in the family tree with the correct name and, in English, the relationship to Mrs Gandolfi. (*Answers on page 126.*)

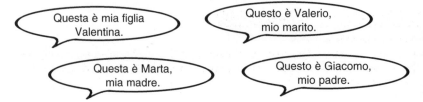

Questa è mia figlia Valentina.

Questo è Valerio, mio marito.

Questa è Marta, mia madre.

Questo è Giacomo, mio padre.

16

A ....
....

B ....
....

C ....
....

Signora Gandolfi

D ....
....

3 My family. Oral practice. Follow the model provided by Mrs Gandolfi to introduce real or imaginary members of your family.

4 Stretch yourself. My family tree. Draw you own family tree in Italian on a separate sheet of paper. Consult your dictionary if you want to include relationships you have not yet learned.

Tip

Italian adjectives (for example **questo, mio, suo**) take the gender (masculine/feminine) of the noun they accompany. Mrs Gandolfi says **questo** when she is referring to her husband/son but **questa** when she is introducing her daughter. She says **mio figlio** ('my son') but **mia figlia** ('my daughter'). It is the gender of the person/object described that determines whether you say **mio** or **mia**. Whether you are a man or a woman, you will always say: **mio padre e mia madre, suo fratello e sua sorella**.

Practise your possessives
Put the correct form of **mio/mia** in front of the following words:

...... marito	...... moglie	...... padre	..... madre	..... figlio	..... figlia
......	......	......	......	......	......

Now do the same with **suo/sua**. (*Answers on page 126.*)
Remember: what matters is not the gender of the possessor but the gender of what is possessed.

Panorama italiano

The Italian family
Contrary to popular myth Italian families are very small. The 1993 census figures show that Italy is the country with the lowest fertility rate in the world (1.3 children per woman).

7 Test yourself

Revision

You have been studying Italian for 6 days, now it is time to do some revision. Use the puzzles and exercises in this Unit to check your progress. You may be surprised by how much you have learned already!

Giochi (Puzzles)

1 Scrambled letters. Daniela Rossetti has spent her first day on the beach in Porto Rotondo writing letters to her family.

Unscramble the words on the envelopes to find to which of her relatives Daniela has written and list them in the left-hand box. Don't forget to unscramble the correct word for **my**. (*Answers on page 126.*)

Daniela intends to write to all the relatives on the Rossetti family tree. List all those she still has to write to, in Italian, in the right-hand box using the correct word for 'her'. (*Answers on page 126.*)

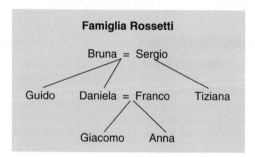

Daniela has written to	Daniela still has to write to
....	....
....	....
....	....
....	

2 Role play. You are Miss Benson and you meet Mr Colombo on an Italian beach. Answer his questions in Italian in the pauses on the recording using the visual prompts below. He starts by saying good morning. (*Answers on page 126.*)

................,
Signor Colombo

3 A night at the opera. Match the phrases in the left-hand column with those on the right. Once you have arranged the right-hand phrases in the correct order, the highlighted letters will give the name of a famous Italian theatre. (*Answers on page 126.*)

1 Come si chiama?	A **S**ì, sono di Boston.
2 È di Venezia?	B Come va?
3 Signora, Lei è americana?	C No, sono **c**ommesso.
4 È insegnante di inglese?	D No, Cosimo è figlio di Letizia.
5 Ciao.	E Sì, **l**avoro in una ditta.
6 Questo è suo figlio?	F No, sono di Ferr**a**ra.
7 Lavora in una ditta?	G **L**uciano Pavarotti.

4 Crossword Puzzle. Write your answers in Italian; the letters in the shaded column will give you the Italian name of a famous city. (*Answers on page 126.*)

Clues   **1** the opposite of **sì**   **2** also   **3** reply to **grazie**   **4** factory worker
5 work   **6** I

5 Around the world in Italian. Listen to the recording. Do you recognize the Italian names of the following countries? Next to each country write its sequence number from the recording. (*Answers on page 126.*)

A Australia	E Belgium	I Canada	M China
B France	F Germany	J Holland	N Ireland
C Japan	G Norway	K Portugal	O Spain
D Sweden	H Switzerland	L United States	P Wales

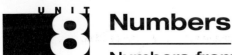

Numbers

Numbers from 0 to 19

Vocabolario

anno	year
anni	years
casa	house
prefisso	code
chiave	key
numero	number
tempo	time
da quanto tempo	since when, how long
da dieci anni	for ten years, since ten years ago
subito	immediately
il	the (m)
mi dispiace	I'm sorry
fa (fare)	you do, you have been doing
abita (abitare)	you live

0	zero	5	cinque	10	dieci	15	quindici
1	uno	6	sei	11	undici	16	sedici
2	due	7	sette	12	dodici	17	diciassette
3	tre	8	otto	13	tredici	18	diciotto
4	quattro	9	nove	14	quattordici	19	diciannove

Dialoghi

Marco tries to ring Paola but gets the wrong number.

Marco	Pronto, Paola?
Signora Brambilla	Scusi? Qui è casa Brambilla.
Marco	È il tre cinque sette, zero otto sei?
Signora Brambilla	No, mi dispiace. Questo è il tre quattro sette, zero otto sei. Prefisso per Roma zero sei.
Marco	Grazie e scusi.

At the hotel reception Mrs Cacciari asks for her key.

Signora Cacciari	Chiave numero dodici, per favore.
Reception	Subito, signora Cacciari.

Mr Varchi is at an interview.

Interviewer	Signor Varchi, da quanto tempo fa questo lavoro?
Signor Varchi	Da dieci anni.
Interviewer	Da quanto tempo abita a Milano?
Signor Varchi	Da un anno.

1 Listen to the recording. Write down the missing telephone numbers and correct the others. (*Answers on page 126.*)

2 Discover the six hidden numbers. (*Answers on page 126.*)

O	A	P	S	E	I	R	C	A	X	U
S	T	P	D	I	C	I	O	T	T	O
S	E	T	Q	U	I	N	D	I	C	I
D	I	P	O	D	C	I	N	Q	U	E
Z	R	L	D	O	D	I	C	I	T	H

3 Listen to four questions and answer them following the prompts below and on the recording. (*Answers on page 126.*)

1. Say 'for three years'.   **2.** Say 'for eighteen years'.   **3.** Say 'No, key number fourteen'.   **4.** Say 'No, this is 570 342; code 01475'.

The third person singular verb form is the same as that used with the polite form of 'you':

Lei è italiano.	You are Italian.
Il numero è ...	The number is ...

This is true for all verbs.

Maria abita a Milano.	Maria lives in Milan.
Lei abita a Milano?	Do you live in Milan?

When the number **uno** (one) is followed by a noun, it behaves like the indefinite article and takes different endings:

un anno	one/a year	**uno studente**	one/a student
una chiave	one/a key	**un'amica**	one/a friend (f)

The telephone
There are different area codes according to the city and province. Here are some. Roma 06, Milano 02, Firenze 055, Venezia 041, Napoli 081.

The local codes are an integral part of Italian telephone numbers and must be dialled even when calling within the same area.

The number for the emergency services is 113.

Numbers

Numbers from 20 to 2000

 Vocabolario

quanto?	how much?
costa (costare)	it costs
borsetta	handbag
borsellino	purse
abito (abitare)	I live
via	street
invece	instead
interno	flat number
giorno	day
oggi	today
che giorno è oggi?	what is the date today?
compleanno	birthday
quando?	when?
primo	first
gennaio	January
febbraio	February
marzo	March

20	venti	40	quaranta	90	novanta
21	ventuno	50	cinquanta	100	cento
22	ventidue	60	sessanta	200	duecento
28	ventotto	70	settanta	1000	mille
30	trenta	80	ottanta	2000	duemila

 Dialoghi

Mr Carnaghi enquires about prices.

Signor Carnaghi	Quanto costa questa borsetta?
Shop assistant	Cinquantatremila lire.
Signor Carnaghi	E questo borsellino?
Shop assistant	Trentacinquemila.

Marcello and Paola exchange addresses.

Marcello	Io abito in Via Mazzini quarantasette.
Paola	Io invece abito in Via Venticinque Aprile quaranta, interno centotrentuno.

A few questions about dates.

Paola	Che giorno è oggi?
Signor Bosi	È il ventinove marzo.
Paola	Quando è il suo compleanno?
Signor Bosi	Il trenta gennaio.

Esercizi

1 Listen to the recording and write in Italian the numbers mentioned. (*Answers on page 126.*)

....

....

....

2 Match each written number with its numeral. (*Answers on page 126.*)

A milletrecentoventidue	**1**	20400
B settecentotré	**2**	78
C novecentocinquantasette	**3**	703
D settantotto	**4**	66
E sessantasei	**5**	957
F ventimilaquattrocento	**6**	1322

3 You are playing **tombola** (Italian bingo) with some friends. Call out the following numbers in Italian. (*Answers on page 126.*)

   (13)

Tip

Dates take the article **il** in front of the cardinal number ('two', 'three', etc.) and the article **l'** in front of **otto** and **undici**:

il tre marzo   the third of March
il due febbraio   the second of February
l'otto agosto   the eighth of August
l'undici novembre   the eleventh of November

The only exception is the first of the month:

il primo gennaio   the first of January

The names of the months are not capitalized.

Cento ('one hundred') and **mille** ('one thousand') are never preceded by the Italian for 'one' as they are in English. When **cento** follows other numbers it does not change. **Mille**, however, changes to **mila**:

cinquecento   500   **duemilacinquecento**   2500

When **tre** (three) is the last digit of a larger number it takes an accent.

ventitré   23   **centotré**   103

Panorama italiano

In Italy playing lotto (**la lotteria**) is a long-standing tradition. Throughout the year there are various TV games linked to the lotto. In certain parts of Italy it is a 'tradition' to interpret dreams and play the numbers that the dreams represent. *La Smorfia* is a well known book from Naples, giving a detailed list of dreams and the numbers associated with them. Another traditional game is **tombola** (a type of bingo) played within the family.

People

Filling in forms

 Vocabolario

pronto soccorso	first-aid post
nome	first name
cognome	surname
di nome	by first name
di cognome	by surname
nazionalità	nationality
capisco (capire)	I understand
non	not
non capisco	I don't understand
residenza	place of residence
indirizzo	address
dove	where
a	in (used for towns)
professione	occupation
da solo	alone, by oneself (m)
da sola	alone, by oneself (f)
con	with
gruppo	party

Dialogo

Mr Brooks has had a skiing accident in Courmayeur and has been taken to the **pronto soccorso** (first-aid post) where he is being asked for his personal details.

Nurse	Come si chiama?
Mr Brooks	James Brooks.
Nurse	James di nome e Brooks di cognome?
Mr Brooks	Sì.
Nurse	Nazionalità?
Mr Brooks	Scusi, non capisco.
Nurse	È americano?
Mr Brooks	Oh no, io non sono americano, sono inglese.
Nurse	Residenza?
Mr Brooks	Scusi, non capisco.
Nurse	Indirizzo? Dove abita?
Mr Brooks	Qui, a Courmayeur?
Nurse	No, in Inghilterra.
Mr Brooks	29 South Street, Cottingham, Yorkshire.
Nurse	Professione?
Mr Brooks	Insegnante.
Nurse	È qui da solo?
Mr Brooks	No, non sono qui da solo, sono con un gruppo di Cottingham High School.

Esercizi

1   Identification. Match the personal details with the right person. (*Answers on page 126.*)

A	B	C	D

1 Nazionalità: americana   1 _____
2 Data di nascita: 2/9/98   2 _____
3 Professione: segretaria, Hotel Valdigne 3 _____
4 Professione: calciatore   4 _____

2 Form filling. Listen to the recording and complete the grid below. (*Answers on page 126.*)

	1	2
Nome		
Cognome		
Nazionalità		
Residenza		
Professione		

3 Guess the questions. Read these negative answers and write the questions in Italian. (*Answers on page 126.*)

A No, non sono Madonna.
B No, non sono cinese.
C No, Courmayeur non è in Francia.
D No, questo non è il pronto soccorso.
E No, non sono qui da sola.

4 Practise saying 'No'. Listen to the recording and reply following the prompts below and on the recording. (*Answers on page 126.*)

1. Say 'No, I'm not John Travolta'.   **2.** Say 'No, Maria is not in London'.
3. Say, 'No, Cosimo is not in Italy.   **4.** Say, 'No, I'm not with a group'.

Tip

In Italian the negative **non** always precedes the verb.
In negative answers, the word order is **no** + **non** + verb;

| **No, non sono americano.** | No, I am not American. |

If the subject pronoun is used, it is placed between **no** and **non**:

| **No, io non mi chiamo Laura.** | No, my name isn't Laura. |

In statements you use just **non** + verb: **non capisco.**

Italian uses **in** with the names of countries but **a** with the names of towns:

| **Sono a Venezia, in Italia.** | I am in Venice, Italy. |

Panorama italiano

Italy is a very bureaucratic country, where people are expected to fill in many more official forms than in some other parts of the world. This can be done very quickly provided you are familiar with the terminology.

Food and drink

Getting a snack

Vocabolario

desidera? (desiderare)	what would you like? (*asked by cashier, waitress, etc.*)
cappuccino	cappuccino
aranciata	orangeade
panino	roll
formaggio	cheese
brioche	bun
allora	right then
in tutto	all together
resto	change
lo	the (m)
scontrino	payment slip
poi	then
del, dello	some
ghiaccio	ice
vorrei (volere)	I would like
zucchero	sugar

Dialoghi

At the till of a coffee bar Mr De Luca pays for some drinks and snacks before going to the bar, to order them.

Cashier	Desidera?
Signor De Luca	Un cappuccino, una coca, un'aranciata, un panino al formaggio e due brioche.
Cashier	Allora, un cappuccino 2000, una coca 2000, un'aranciata 2000, un panino al formaggio 3000, due brioche 4000; 13.000 lire in tutto.
Signor De Luca	Ecco 20.000 lire.
Cashier	Ecco il resto e lo scontrino.
Signor De Luca	Grazie.
Cashier	Grazie a Lei.

Having paid, Mr De Luca now orders the drinks at the bar.

Waitress	Desidera?
Signor De Luca	Un cappuccino ...
Waitress	Lo scontrino, per favore.
Signor De Luca	Ecco lo scontrino.
Waitress	Grazie, allora un cappuccino, e poi?
Signor De Luca	Una coca e un'aranciata.
Waitress	Desidera del ghiaccio?
Signor De Luca	No, grazie, ma vorrei dello zucchero.

Tip

Dealing with large numbers can be confusing. Learn what 5000, 10,000, 50,000, 100,000, 1,000,000 lire are approximately equivalent to in your own currency before you leave for Italy.

Esercizi

1 Match and draw. Match the three pictures with the items on the payment slip. Draw the other two in the blank squares and write in English what they are. (*Answers on page 126.*)

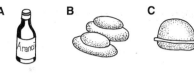

Bar dell'aeroporto	
1 1 aranciata	£2000
2 1 panino	£3000
3 1 espresso	£2000
4 2 brioche	£4000
5 1 birra	£5000
TOTALE	£16.000

A

B

C

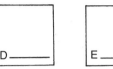

D _____ E _____

A _____

B _____

C _____

2 Listen to the recording. Pretend to be the waiter and write down in Italian your customers' orders. (*Answers on page 126.*)

A ....

B ....

C ....

3 Your turn to order. Order the items shown below. Start each request with **Vorrei ...** and end with **per favore**. (*Answers on pages 126–27.*)

A   B   C   D   E

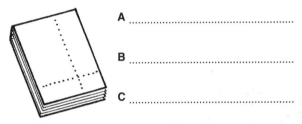

Tip

The definite article ('the') is **il** before most singular masculine nouns: *il* **bambino,** *il* **calciatore.**
Before singular masculine nouns which start with **z-** or **s-** + consonant it is *lo*: *lo* **scontrino.**
To say 'some' or 'any' in Italian you can use the partitive article, **del** in front of nouns that take the article **il**, **dello** in front of nouns that take the article **lo**:

del ghiaccio	some ice
dello zucchero	some sugar

Panorama italiano

In Italian bars and cafes you can consume your food and drinks standing at the bar or sitting at a table. If you stand you pay for what you want at the till and then give the waiter your payment slip together with your order. This is what the sign **scontrino alla cassa** displayed in many bars means. If you sit at a table you will pay more. Also cafes in resorts make an additional charge if they have live music.

 **Travel**

At the railway station

la	the (f)
l'	the (m and f)
il treno	train
per	to, for
il binario	platform
al binario …	on platform …
dov'è …?	where is …?
la carrozza	carriage
il ristorante	restaurant
la carrozza ristorante	dining car
in coda	at the rear
in testa	at the front
la classe	class
dopo	after
primo, prima	first
secondo, seconda	second
l'orario	timetable
subito dopo	immediately after
il gabinetto	toilet
il treno delle dieci	the ten o'clock train

Note that from this Unit nouns included in the **Vocabolario** are given with the definite article.

 Dialoghi

Mrs Richmond is looking for her train.

Mrs Richmond	Scusi, il treno per Padova?
Attendant	Il treno per Padova è al binario numero 2.
Mrs Richmond	Dov'è la carrozza ristorante?
Attendant	La carrozza ristorante è in testa dopo la prima classe.

Paul McPherson is looking for the second class carriages.

Paul McPherson	Scusi, dov'è la seconda classe?
Attendant	La seconda classe è in coda; la prima classe è in testa.
Paul McPherson	E scusi, dov'è l'orario?
Attendant	L'orario è lì, subito dopo il pronto soccorso.

Tip

To understand station announcements familiarize yourself with the Italian names of the following towns: **Firenze** ('Florence'), **Genova** ('Genoa'), **Milano** ('Milan'), **Padova** ('Padua'), **Torino** ('Turin'), **Venezia** ('Venice'), **Napoli** ('Naples').

Esercizi

1 Trains and stations. Read the six answers and work out the questions in English. (*Answers on page 127.*)

    A La carrozza ristorante è dopo la seconda classe.
    B Il gabinetto è dopo questa carrozza.
    C Il treno per Napoli è al binario otto.
    D No, questa non è la prima classe.
    E La seconda classe è in coda.
    F Il pronto soccorso è al binario quattro.

2 Stretch yourself. Now ask the questions in Esercizio 1 in Italian. (*Answers on page 127.*)

3 You are at the railway station in Milan. Listen to the recorded announcements and complete in English the timetable below. (*Answers on page 127.*)

	Destination	Platform	Other information
A			
B			
C			
D			
E			

4 Use the visual prompts below to ask questions beginning with **Scusi, dov'è … ?** Also, write down a reply to each question in Italian on a separate sheet of paper. (*Answers on page 127.*)

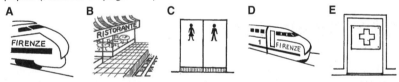

Tip

The definite article is **la** in front of singular feminine nouns: *la* **carrozza**, *la* **classe**. It is **l'** in front of singular masculine and feminine nouns which start with **a-, e-, i-, o-, u-**:

*l'***orario** (m), *l'***indirizzo** (m), *l'***aranciata** (f), *l'***Italia** (f)

You can use either **binario uno/due**, etc. or **primo/secondo binario**, etc. to refer to platforms.

Panorama italiano

In spite of myths to the contrary, the Italian train service is efficient and trains run on time. There are however occasions, such as the Easter period and the month of August when trains become very crowded. Then it is well worth using the fastest and most expensive trains; these can have striking names such as Romolo or Marco Polo.

13 Numbers

Expressing age

la foto	photograph
l'anno	year
il mese	month
chi?	who?
il bambino	child (m)
la bambina	child (f)
il/la cantante	singer (m and f)
adesso	now
ho	I have
ha (avere)	he/she/it has
il tempo	time
come passa il tempo!	time flies!
di tre anni	of three years, three-year-old
basta	enough
solo	only, just

Dialoghi

Mrs Forni and Mrs Bettini are talking about their children.

Signora Forni Luca ha solo sette anni e Giorgia ha quindici mesi.
Signora Bettini Io ho tre figli: Sergio di sedici anni, Daniela di diciannove e Marina di quindici.

Fausto and Silvia are visiting their friend Graziella and looking at old photographs.

Graziella Ecco Chiara, la figlia di Paolo: in questa foto ha cinque anni.
Fausto E chi è questo bambino?
Silvia Questo è suo fratello Lorenzo.
Fausto Adesso la figlia di Paolo ha due bambine di tre e sei anni.
Silvia E Lorenzo ha un figlio di nove anni.
Graziella Come passa il tempo!
Silvia Graziella, chi è questa bambina?
Graziella Sono io, ma basta, basta foto!

Tip

Practise your numbers! Make use of those idle moments when you are waiting for the bus or travelling by train. Think of the Italian for the numbers you see on licence plates and in advertisements.

Esercizi

1 How many of each? Write out in full how many people or things there are in each picture. (*Answers on page 127.*)

A ...... commesse   **B** .... bambini   **C** .... foto   **D** .... segretarie

2   Phone numbers. Listen to the recording and write down the sequences of numbers. Use numerals. (*Answers on page 127.*)

> A ....
> B ....
> C ....
> D ....

3   Rewind the recording and repeat each sequence in Italian, as if you were checking it.

4   Write a sentence to say how old each child is. The first one has been done for you.

Paola	7 (years)	Paola ha sette anni.
Marco	3 (years)	....
Gianni	10 (months)	....
Marina	4 (years)	....
Vieri	2 (years)	....
Anna	6 (months)	....

Tip

Age is expressed by means of the verb **avere** ('to have'):

Paolo ha cinque anni. Paolo is five years old. (*literally*) Paolo *has* five years.

The plural ending of masculine nouns which end in **-o** is **-i**.
The plural ending of feminine nouns which end in **-a** is **-e**.
The plural ending of all nouns which end in **-e** is **-i**:

un anno due anni una bambina due bambine un/una cantante due cantanti

Abbreviated words keep the gender of the original word: **foto** comes from **fotografia** and so remains feminine.
Abbreviated and foreign words do not change in the plural:

una foto   due foto   una brioche   due brioche

First names which end in **-i** are usually male: **Gianni, Vieri**.

Panorama italiano

Numbers
This is how Italians handwrite the figures 1, 4 and 7:

Test yourself

Revision

You are now ready to revise and consolidate the vocabulary and language structures you have encountered in Units 8–13.

Giochi

1 Only a matter of words! You have just arrived at the campsite, and the receptionist is filling in a form with your personal details. Use the personal details given below to answer the receptionist's questions. (*Answers on page 127.*)

Robert McClaren	Scottish	35 Main Street, Glasgow	engineer

2 Hunting for numbers. Find Sara Cantoni's age and birthday in this wordsearch.

D	I	C	I	A	S	S	E	T	T	E
A	B	D	O	D	I	C	I	U	V	M
S	T	O	T	T	R	C	L	P	B	N
S	M	A	R	Z	O	F	G	Z	S	N

Now you have found the answers, ask the questions in Italian.
(*Answers on page 127.*)

3 The octopus. Look at the word in each octopus face and then write five related words using the visual prompts. (*Answers on page 127.*)

4 Tidying up. Put the words below under the correct form of the definite article. (*Answers on page 127.*)

il	la	l'	lo

scontrino	binario	orario	gabinetto	indirizzo	cognome	studente

classe	carrozza	aranciata	brioche	coca cola	bambino	zero

foto	tempo	borsetta	ristorante	zucchero	amica

5 A trip to Rome. Match the questions with the answers. Once you have arranged the right-hand phrases in the correct order, write down the first letter of each reply to find the name of the fastest and most modern train from Milan to Rome. (*Answers on page 127.*)

1	Prima o seconda classe?	**A** Ottavia.	☐
2	Ecco 30.000.	**B** Lire.	☐
3	È italiano?	**C** No, sono americano.	☐
4	Desidera?	**D** In coda.	☐
5	Quando?	**E** Oggi.	☐
6	In tutto trentacinquemila …	**F** Ecco il resto.	☐
7	Dov'è la carrozza ristorante?	**G** Due brioche e due caffè.	☐
8	Da quanto tempo fa questo lavoro?	**H** Nove anni.	☐
9	Come si chiama questa bambina?	**I** Prima.	☐

6 The odd-one-out. Which word has nothing in common with the others? (*Answers on page 127.*)

A	numero	prefisso	otto	scuola
B	via	indirizzo	residenza	orario
C	prima	seconda	scontrino	classe

7 One too many. Write down the plural of the following words. (*Answers on page 127.*)

e.g. un bambino	due	bambini
un cappuccino	due	....
una brioche	due	....
un'aranciata	due	....
un treno	due	....
un anno	due	....
una foto	due	....

8 The end of Chiara's holiday. Fill in the gaps using the list of words given below. (*Answers on page 127.*)

Chiara è la figlia .... Roberto, ... ingegnere .... Torino. Chiara .... tre anni. Chiara è .... vacanza a Sanremo con la .... e il papà. È al bar della stazione.
'.......... ?' Chiara desidera un panino e .... coca: 'Quanto .... ? 'Ecco il .... ' 'Grazie.' ' .... '
'Il treno .... Torino è .... binario due.' 'Mamma, ... è il gabinetto?'
'È .... testa al treno, Chiara.'

Desidera	di	mamma	ha	costa	dov'	in	un	resto	in	una

al	Prego	di	per

9 Words to pictures. Ask an appropriate question for each picture. Then check your questions against those on the recording. (*Answers on page 127.*)

Travel

Passport control and baggage reclaim

 ### Vocabolario

il passaporto	passport
quanto? quanta?	how much?
quanti? quante?	how many?
quanto tempo?	how long?
la settimana	week
la valigia (le valigie or le valige)	suitcase (suitcases)
pesa (pesare)	it weighs
quanto pesa!	it weighs so much!
rimane (rimanere)	you stay
il carrello	trolley
va (andare)	you go, he/she/it goes
va bene	all right (*literally* it goes well)
andate (andare)	you go (*for more than one person*)
andate pure	you may go
siete (essere)	you are (*for more than one person*)
insieme	together
lì	there

Note that a difficult plural is given here in brackets (…).

Dialoghi

Mr and Mrs Richmond have landed at Marco Polo airport in Venice, and are going through passport control.

Official	Passaporto, prego.
Mrs Richmond	Ecco il mio passaporto.
Official	Quanto tempo rimane in Italia?
Mrs Richmond	Due settimane.
Official	Dove va?
Mrs Richmond	A Venezia e a Firenze.
Mr Richmond	E questo è il mio passaporto.
Official	Siete insieme?
Mr Richmond	Sì, sono suo marito.
Official	Va bene, andate pure.

After passport control, Mr and Mrs Richmond collect their luggage.

Mrs Richmond	Ecco la mia valigia.
Mr Richmond	Quanto pesa!
Mrs Richmond	Scusi, dov'è un carrello?
Traveller	C'è un carrello lì.
Mrs Richmond	Grazie!
Traveller	Prego.

Tip

Many English words derive from Latin and resemble Italian words in sound and meaning. If you do not know the meaning of a word it is worth venturing a guess!

1 Match each picture with the appropriate exclamation. (*Answers on page 127.*)

A Quanti figli!

C Quante valigie!

B Quanto lavoro!

D Quanti carrelli!

1   2   3   4

2 Something missing. Listen to the first dialogue again and add the missing words without looking back at the text. (*Answers on page 127.*)

A .... tempo rimane in Italia?   **B** .... va?

C .... insieme?   **D** .... bene, ... pure.

3 Role play. You are Mr Richmond. Listen to the recording and answer in Italian using the visual prompts below. To begin with you are asked for your passport. (*Answers on page 127.*)

A   **B**   **C**   **D**

Tip

A different form of the verb (the plural) is used to address more than one person: è 'you are' (for one person), **siete** 'you are' (for more than one person).

When the question word **quanto** accompanies a noun it agrees with it (masculine singular **quanto** and plural **quanti**; feminine singular **quanta** and plural **quante**). When it accompanies a verb the form **quanto** is used:

Quanto pesa!   How heavy it is!

The article **il, lo, la,** etc. is used in Italian in front of the possessive:

il mio passaporto   my passport   **la mia valigia**   my suitcase

However, singular words which denote family relationships (see Unit 6) are an exception: **mia madre, suo fratello**.

Panorama italiano

Travelling with young children
Italian airports are well provided with services for adult holidaymakers and business people, but lack facilities for children. Where there are changing facilities, they are very basic (the same is true of railway stations and department stores). Baby food and nappies are readily available in supermarkets and at chemists; the brand names are well known and the quality is the same as in most northern European countries.

People

The extended family

Vocabolario

i, gli	the (m pl)
le	the (f pl)
cosa?	what?
faccio (fare)	I do, I make
Pasqua	Easter
passo (passare)	I spend (time)
la casa	house
a casa	at home
la zia	aunt
lo zio	uncle
la cugina (le cugine)	cousin (cousins) (f)
il cugino (i cugini)	cousin (cousins) (m)
il nipote (i nipoti)	nephew (nephews)
la nipote (le nipoti)	niece (nieces)
il parente (i parenti)	relative (relatives)
il pranzo	dinner
tutti	all
la famiglia	family
in famiglia	with the family

Dialogo

Mrs Sgorbato and Mrs Martini talk about their plans for Easter.

Signora Sgorbato	Signora Martini, cosa fa per Pasqua?
Signora Martini	Passo la Pasqua a casa, in famiglia.
Signora Sgorbato	Ha fratelli e sorelle?
Signora Martini	No, ma ho due zie: la zia Laura e la zia Silvia; due zii: lo zio Paolo e lo zio Mario; tre cugine e sei nipoti.
Signora Sgorbato	Quanti parenti, signora Martini!
Signora Martini	Sì, e quest'anno il pranzo di Pasqua è a casa mia.
Signora Sgorbato	E Lei fa il pranzo di Pasqua per le zie, gli zii, le cugine e tutti i nipoti?
Signora Martini	Sì, io faccio il pranzo per tutti.
Signora Sgorbato	Quanto lavoro, signora Martini!

Esercizi

1 Write in the missing words. (*Answers on page 127.*)

C cugini
zii ←――→ zie
....

D figli
fratelli ←――→ ....
figlie

2 Listen to the recording and join up the four people with the illustrations below. (*Answers on page 127.*)

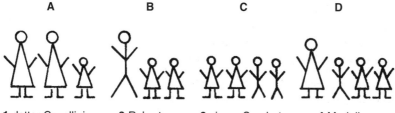

A   B   C   D

1 dottor Cavallini   **2** Roberta   **3** signor Sgorbato   **4** Mariella

3 Role play. Listen to the recording and imagine you are Mrs Martini. Tell Mr Sgorbato about your plans for Easter. He speaks first. Follow the prompts below. (*Answers on page 127.*)

1. Say 'I am spending Easter at home'.   **2.** Say 'Yes, this year I am making the Easter dinner'.   **3.** Say 'Yes, for all the relatives: for two uncles, three nephews and five cousins'.

Tip

The table below shows the plural forms of the definite article:

	Masc			*Fem*	
Sing	**il**	**lo**	**l'**	**la**	**l'**
Pl	**i**	**gli**	**gli**	**le**	**le**

When sons and daughters, uncles and aunts, nephews and nieces, male and female cousins are mentioned together, the masculine plural form is used, e.g. **i figli** can include daughters as well as sons, **gli zii** can include aunts as well as uncles.

The verb **fare** is irregular. Learn the different forms as you meet them.

Panorama italiano

Easter time is for travelling! Many families visit their relatives living in different towns. There is much regional variation in the food served for a traditional Easter breakfast or lunch but you can count on rich cakes and brightly coloured hard-boiled eggs. Families organize egg hunts for the children. On Easter Monday picnics are a very popular activity.

Vocabolario

ora	hour
sono	they are
che ora è?	what time is it?
che ore sono?	what time is it?
a che ora?	at what time?
il telegiornale	news on TV
il canale	channel
sul primo canale	on channel 1
comincia (cominciare)	he/she/it begins
terzo	third
mezzogiorno	midday
mezzanotte	midnight
l'una	one o'clock
di mattina	in the morning
di pomeriggio (or) del pomeriggio	in the afternoon
di sera	in the evening
di notte	in the night
... e mezzo (or) e mezza	half past ...
... e un quarto	quarter past ...
... e tre quarti	quarter to ...
parlare	to speak
la riunione	meeting
ritorna (ritornare)	he/she/it comes/goes back
l'ufficio	office
parte (partire)	he/she/it leaves
il traghetto	ferry
di solito	usually, normally

Dialoghi

Paola wishes to watch the news.

Paola   Scusi, che ora è, per favore?
Signor Bosi   È mezzogiorno e un quarto.
Paola   A che ora è il telegiornale?
Signor Bosi   Sul primo canale alle dodici e trenta, sul secondo alle tredici e sul terzo alle quattordici.

Michael wants to know at what time school starts in Italy.

Michael   A che ora comincia la scuola in Italia?
Gabriella   In Italia la scuola comincia alle otto di mattina.

Mrs Snelgrove needs to contact Doctor Vassi, so she rings up his office.

Mrs Snelgrove   Pronto, vorrei parlare con il dottor Vassi.
Secretary   Mi dispiace, il dottor Vassi non è in ufficio.
Mrs Snelgrove   A che ora ritorna?
Secretary   Il dottor Vassi è in riunione fino a mezzogiorno, di solito ritorna in ufficio verso le quattro, quattro e un quarto del pomeriggio.

1   Match the times. Match clocks 1–4 with the right time. Then complete the faces of the two blank clocks with the times left over. (*Answers on page 127.*)

A le otto   **B** le due e un quarto   **C** le undici e cinquanta
D le sei e tre quarti   **E** l'una e dieci   **F** mezzanotte

2   The speaking clock. Listen to the recording which uses the 24-hour clock. Write down in numerals the times you hear, adding a.m. and p.m. (*Answers on page 127.*)

   A _____   **B** _____   **C** _____   **D** _____   **E** _____

3   Your turn to tell the time. Match the questions with the answers and read them aloud. (*Answers on page 127.*)

   1. Dov'è il treno delle ventidue zero quattro per Milano?
   2. Che ora è?
   3. A che ora parte il volo per Roma?
   4. A che ora ritorna a Messina il traghetto?

   A Il volo per Roma parte alle diciassette e venticinque.
   B Il treno per Milano delle ventidue zero quattro è al secondo binario.
   C Il traghetto ritorna a Messina alle sedici e trentasei.
   D È mezzogiorno e mezza.

Tip

sono can mean both 'I am' and 'they are':

Sono Gianni.	I am Gianni.
I tavoli sono prenotati.	The tables are booked.

The time can be asked using either of the two expressions **che ora è?** and **che ore sono?** The reply is **sono le** + the number. The words **ora** and **ore** are used only in the question.

Che ora è? What time is it?	**Sono le dodici e venti.** It is twenty past twelve.

e is omitted in formal announcements containing **zero** (0):

il treno delle quindici zero otto	the fifteen o eight train

When giving the time the verb is always plural (**sono** ...), except with the three expressions:

È mezzogiorno. It is midday. **È mezzanotte.** It is midnight. **È l'una.** It is one o'clock.

There are no expressions equivalent to a.m. or p.m. To be specific, Italians add 'in the morning', etc: **le cinque di mattina, l'una di notte.**

Panorama italiano

The 24-hour clock is used on timetables and in formal situations; the 12-hour clock is used informally. The school and work day is slightly different than in some other countries. Schools and offices normally start at 8 o'clock and in the smaller centres people return home for lunch and go back to work in the afternoon.

Food and drink

Booking a table

Vocabolario

pronto	hello (*on phone*)
la pizzeria	pizza restaurant
prenotare	to book
il tavolo	table
chiuso, chiusa	closed
va bene	it is all right
per quanti?	for how many?
all'aperto	outdoors
sono (essere)	they are
tutto, tutta, tutti, tutte	all
prenotato, prenotata	booked
la sala	dining room
da asporto	to take away
pesto	sauce of basil, pinenuts, olive oil, garlic, Pecorino cheese
lunedì	Monday
martedì	Tuesday
mercoledì	Wednesday
giovedì	Thursday
venerdì	Friday
sabato	Saturday
domenica	Sunday

Dialogo

Mr and Mrs Martinelli want to take Paul McPherson out to eat an excellent pizza. Mr Martinelli calls Pizzeria Marechiaro to book a table.

Signor Martinelli	Pronto, 040-83-37-47?
Proprietor	Sì, pronto, Pizzeria Marechiaro.
Signor Martinelli	Vorrei prenotare un tavolo per giovedì sera.
Proprietor	Mì dispiace, giovedì la pizzeria è chiusa.
Signor Martinelli	Sabato allora.
Proprietor	Sì, sabato va bene. Per quanti?
Signor Martinelli	Per tre. Vorrei un tavolo all'aperto.
Proprietor	I tavoli all'aperto sono tutti prenotati, ma ho un tavolo in sala.
Signor Martinelli	Va bene, allora in sala.
Proprietor	Il suo nome prego?
Signor Martinelli	MARTINELLI.
Proprietor	Va bene allora, signor Martinelli, un tavolo per tre per sabato sera.
Signor Martinelli	Sì, va bene, buona sera e grazie.
Proprietor	Buona sera.

Esercizi

1   Taking orders. To improve your Italian you have found a summer job in Italy, taking telephone orders for Pizzeria Marechiaro. Listen to the recording and write down in English what dottor Giovannini orders. (*Answers on page 127.*)

2 Describe a pizza. Are you familiar with the dishes dottor Giovannini has ordered? Write the main ingredients in English for each type of pizza and for this particular spaghetti sauce. If you don't know check in an Italian cookery book. (*Answers on page 127.*)

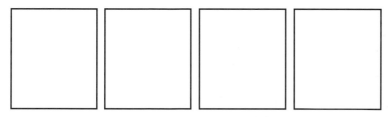

3 Your turn to book. Ring up Pizzeria Romana to book a table. Listen to the recording and speak in the gaps, using the prompts provided below. You speak first. (*Answers on page 127.*)

1. Say 'Hello, Pizzeria Romana?' **2.** Say 'I'd like to book a table for Friday evening'. **3.** Say 'Outdoors please'. **4.** Say 'For four'. **5.** Say your name. **6.** Say 'Yes, thank you'.

Tip

The first day of the week is **lunedì** ('Monday') and the last is **domenica** ('Sunday'). Note that the names of the days are not capitalized.

Adjectives are words that describe nouns. You have already met some Italian adjectives, those describing nationalities (Unit 3), and possessives (Unit 6). Many adjectives have four possible endings. These are the same as those of nouns which end in **-o** and **-a**:

tavol*o* prenotat*o*	tavol*i* prenotat*i*
pizzeri*a* chius*a*	pizzeri*e* chius*e*

Adjectives which end in **-e** in the singular end in **-i** in the plural:

zuppa ingles*e*	trifle	**zuppe ingles*i***	trifles

Panorama italiano

To make tax evasion difficult, restaurants and shops, including shops which provide services like hairdressers or rent out items such as skis, are required by law to give you, upon payment, a receipt called a **ricevuta fiscale**. While you are still near the premises you must keep this receipt and have it available for inspection, otherwise you may be fined.

Time matters

Opening and closing times

 ## Vocabolario

da	from
dalle	from (*followed by times*)
dal	from the, on the
alle	to (*followed by times*)
la banca (le banche)	bank (banks)
il tipo	type
il negozio	shop
il supermercato	supermarket
apre (aprire)	it opens
riapre (riaprire)	it opens again
aprono	they open
chiude (chiudere)	it closes
chiudono	they close
dipende da (dipendere)	it depends on
l'orario di apertura	opening times
l'orario di chiusura	closing times
tranne	except for

 ## Dialoghi

Mr Ford needs to change money. He enquires about the opening times of banks.

Mr Ford — Scusi, a che ora apre la banca?
Clerk — La banca apre dalle otto e trenta alle dodici e quarantacinque e poi riapre per un'ora.
Mr Ford — E a che ora riapre?
Clerk — Riapre dalle quattordici e trenta alle quindici e trenta.

Mrs Walters wants to go shopping. She enquires about closing times.

Mrs Walters — Scusi, a che ora chiudono i negozi?
Assistant — Dipende dal tipo di negozio. Di solito chiudono alle venti, venti e trenta.

Mr Boldi asks about the opening times of supermarkets.

Signor Boldi — Scusi, a che ora aprono i supermercati?
Assistant — Dipende dal giorno. Di solito aprono alle nove, tranne il lunedì, quando aprono alle quattordici.

Esercizi

 1 Listen to the recording and insert the opening and closing times of these two places. (*Answers on page 127.*)

2 Complete the puzzle. The shaded vertical column will give you the name of an Italian shop. (*Answers on page 127.*)

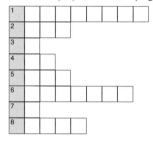

Clues **1** Italian for 'cheese' **2** La banca apre dalle 8.30 ... 12.45. **3** ... in front of 'aprire' means 'again'. **4** 'my' in front of 'fratello' **5** Il supermercato ... alle 9.00. **6** A che ora ... i negozi la sera? **7** 'the' in front of 'tipo' **8** Italian for 'also'

3 English opening and closing times. Listen to the questions on the recording and reply using the information in the grid below. Use the 24-hour clock. (*Answers on page 127.*)

	Orario	
	apertura	chiusura
Banche	9.30	16.30
Supermercati	9.00	20.00
Negozi	9.00	17.00–17.30

Tip

When **da** ('from') and **a** ('to') are followed by **il, la, lo, le** ('the') etc., the words combine. Look at the way **a** combines below and do the same for **da** following the same pattern. (*Answers on page 127.*)

	il	lo	l'	i	gli	la	l'	le
a	al	allo	all'	ai	agli	alla	all'	alle
da	....	....	....	....	....	....	....	....

Panorama italiano

Generally only supermarkets and large department stores have adopted European times and do not close at lunch time. All other shops close between 14.00 and 16.00. However, they are open longer in the evening, closing at 8.00–8.30 p.m. In the summer, depending on where you are (mainly in resorts), most shops (but not food shops) remain open until 11.00–12.00 at night.

Numbers

At the bank

Vocabolario

c'è	there is
il cambio	exchange rate
la sterlina	pound sterling
la peseta	peseta
lo yen	yen
il marco	Deutschmark
il franco	franc
la lira	lira
oggi	today
cambiare	to change
bene	well
sul	in the
il giornale	newspaper
la commissione	commission
il documento	document, ID
la carta d'identità	identity card
vuole (volere)	do you want?
la banconota	banknote
si accomodi pure a ...	you may go to ...
lo sportello	counter
il totale	total
cinquemila	five thousand
diecimila	ten thousand
ventimila	twenty thousand
cinquantamila	fifty thousand
centomila	one hundred thousand

Dialoghi

Mr Goldoni has decided to spend two weeks in Great Britain. He goes to the bank to enquire about the exchange rate between the lira and the pound sterling.

Signor Goldoni	Quant'è il cambio della lira con la sterlina oggi?
Bank clerk	Oggi la sterlina è a duemilaseicento e novanta.
Signor Goldoni	Grazie.

Mr Goldoni decides to buy £500.

Signor Goldoni	Vorrei cambiare lire per un totale di cinquecento sterline.
Bank clerk	Bene. Ecco.
Signor Goldoni	Ma sul giornale la sterlina è a duemilaseicento e novanta.
Bank clerk	C'è da pagare una commissione.
Signor Goldoni	Queste banche, eh!
Bank clerk	Ha un documento?
Signor Goldoni	Sì. Ecco la carta d'identità.
Bank clerk	Grazie. Si accomodi pure alla cassa. Sportello tre.
Signor Goldoni	Buongiorno, grazie.

Esercizi

1 Listen to the recording and write down the exchange rate (*virgola* = comma). (*Answers on page 128.*)

sterlina	....
peseta	....
yen	....
franco francese	....
marco tedesco	....

2 Make complete sentences by matching the two halves. (*Answers on page 128.*)

A Prego, si accomodi   **1** per un totale di £500.000 (cinquecentomila lire).
B Quant'è oggi   **2** carta d'identità.
C Ecco la mia   **3** una commissione.
D Vorrei cambiare sterline   **4** allo sportello.
E C'è da pagare   **5** il cambio della sterlina?

3 What is the exchange rate today? Listen to the recording again and answer the questions about the exchange rates following the prompts below. (*Answers on page 128.*)

1. Say 'Today the Deutschmark is 980 lire'.
2. Say 'Today the French Franc is 310 lire'.
3. Say 'In the paper the pound is 2690 lire'.
4. Say 'The yen is 14.76 lire' (for 'point' use *virgola*).
5. Say 'It is at 12.63 lire'.

Tip

c'è means 'there is':

C'è una banca. There is a bank.   **C'è da pagare** ... There is ... to pay.

The symbol for the **lira** is almost the same as that used for the pound sterling. In Italian numbers, points are used to separate thousands and commas are used for decimals:

£10.000 ten thousand lire   **£12,63** twelve point sixty-three lire

In the previous unit, we have seen that **a** and **da** combine with the definite article (**il, la, l', lo,** etc.). The same happens with **di** and **su**. An example with **di** is provided below; note that the **-i** changes to **-e-**. Can you do **su**, which does not change its vowel? (*Answers on page 128.*)

	il	lo	l'	i	gli	la	l'	le
di	del	dello	dell'	dei	degli	della	dell'	delle
su	....	....	....	....	....	....	....	....

Panorama italiano

If you need to change money make sure you take your passport with you to the bank. You will be asked to pay a commission for the transaction. Take plenty of cash with you when out and about in Italy because, despite the widespread use of credit cards and eurocheques, Italians still prefer to be paid in cash. All motorways and nearly all petrol stations accept cash only.

Test yourself

Revision

Giochi

1 At the museum. Fill the gaps, and insert the first letter of each missing word in the grid to reveal the name of an important museum in Florence. (*Answers on page 128.*)

☐ **1** Vorrei .... buon gelato!
☐ **2** Questa è la mia famiglia. Mia mamma, mio papà, mia sorella e mio ....
☐ **3** Quant'è il cambio del .... francese oggi?
☐ **4** .... supermercato apre alle nove.
☐ **5** Marta è la sorella di mio papà, è mia ....
☐ **6** Siete .... ? Sì, sono sua moglie.

2 La danza delle ore. Listen to the recording and use the pictures below to answer the questions. (*Answers on page 128.*)

A   **B**   **C**

3 Listen to the recording and follow the prompts below to complete the three dialogues. In each case you speak second. (*Answers on page 128.*)

A 1. Say 'I would like to change five hundred pounds'. **2.** Say 'Here is (my) passport'. **3.** Ask 'How much is the pound today?'

B 1. Say 'I would like to reserve a table for four'. **2.** Say 'Outside'. **3.** Say 'It's all right'.

C 1. Say 'Here is my passport'. **2.** Say 'Three weeks'. **3.** Say 'Here is my suitcase'.

4 Put the sentences below in the correct order to make the dialogue. (*Answers on page 128.*)

A Arrivederci.
B Ecco. Quant'è il cambio della sterlina oggi?
C Buongiorno.
D 2690.
E Buongiorno. Vorrei cambiare cinquecento sterline.
F Va bene, ha un documento?
G E la commissione quant'è?
H Diecimila lire. Ecco, si accomodi pure alla cassa. Sportello tre. Arrivederci e grazie.

5 Many, many, many ... Insert the correct definite article in front of the following words. (*Answers on page 128.*)

.... gelati   .... zii   .... settimane   .... valige
.... passaporti   .... supermercati .... banche   .... orari

6 Complete the crossword and in the shaded column you will find the Italian word for 'clock' and 'watch'. (*Answers on page 128.*)

Clues 1 Che ... è? **2** Il dottor Vassi ..... in ufficio alle due. **3** La scuola in Italia comincia alle .... **4** .... sera (the) **5** .... di apertura e chiusura **6** Sul ...... la sterlina è 2690 lire. **7** ..... traghetto (the) **8** Che ..... sono?

7 Look at the family tree and complete the sentences below. (*Answers on page 128.*)

MARIO   GINA

GIOVANNI   GEMMA   FEDERICA   GIORGIO

IO   MARTA   MICHELE   BARBARA

1 Marta è mia ....
2 Giovanni è .... di mia mamma. È mio ....
3 Federica è .... di Giorgio. È mia ....
4 Michele e Barbara sono i .... di Marta.
5 Io e Marta siamo le .... di Giovanni, Federica e Giorgio.

8 Write in Italian the questions to go with these answers. (*Answers on page 128.*)

1 ....? Sono le sette e mezza.
2 ....? Ritorna in ufficio alle due.
3 ....? Passo la Pasqua in famiglia.
4 ....? I negozi chiudono alle dodici e trenta.

9 Complete each sentence by using one of the prepositions below. One preposition is used twice. (*Answers on page 128.*)

.... giornale la sterlina è a 2750 lire.
C'è .... pagare una commissione?
Passo le vacanze .... famiglia.
Si accomodi .... cassa.
I negozi aprono .... 8.30 .... 12.45.
Dipende .... tipo di negozio.
Vorrei un tavolo .... aperto.
Vorrei un tavolo per tre .... sala.

| all' | alla | alle |

| da | dalle | dal |

| sul | in | in |

10 Use the visual prompts below to answer the recording. (*Answers on page 128.*)

| 9:00 | 13:30 | 21:30 |

Food and drink

Feeling hungry, thirsty, etc.

 ## Vocabolario

ho	I have
hai	you have (*informal*)
ha	you have (*formal*), he/she/it has
la fame	hunger
la sete	thirst
ho fame	I am hungry
ho sete	I am thirsty
la mamma	mum
il papà	dad
tu	you (*informal*)
il gelato	ice cream
il caffè	coffee
buon, buono, buona	good
cosa prendi?	what will you have?
prendi (prendere)	take, have (*informal*)
prenda	take, have (*formal*)
prendo	I'm having, I'm taking
il sonno	sleep
ho sonno	I feel sleepy
freddo	cold, chilled
caldo	hot
ho freddo	I feel cold
ho caldo	I feel hot

 ## Dialogo

Mr and Mrs De Luca and their daughter Stefania stop at a service area on the motorway.

Signor De Luca	Ho sete.
Stefania	Mamma, io ho fame.
Signor De Luca	E tu, Gabriella, hai fame?
Signora De Luca	No, io prendo un caffè.
Stefania	Papà, io vorrei un buon gelato.
Signor De Luca	Stefania, questi gelati non sono buoni, prendi un panino.
Signora De Luca	E tu, Antonio, cosa prendi?
Signor De Luca	Ho sete e ho sonno.
Signora De Luca	Allora prendi un caffè freddo.
Signor De Luca	Buon'idea, il caffè freddo è buono.

Esercizi

1 Missing words. Complete the sentences using the words given opposite. (*Answers on page 128.*)

  1 Vorrei una birra, ho ....

2 Brrr! Non hai .... ?
3 Stefania, se hai ...., prendi una pizza.
4 Gabriella ha .... Ecco un caffè.
5 Ho ...., vorrei un gelato.

A fame   **B** sete   **C** freddo   **D** caldo   **E** sonno

2   Match the pictures with the exclamations. (*Answers on page 128.*)

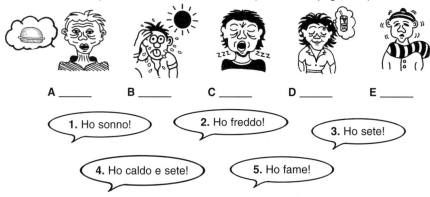

A _____   **B** _____   **C** _____   **D** _____   **E** _____

1. Ho sonno!

2. Ho freddo!

3. Ho sete!

4. Ho caldo e sete!

5. Ho fame!

3   Role play. Listen to the recording and imagine you are Mrs Antonietta Campana. Follow the prompts below, using the **tu** or **Lei** form as appropriate. (*Answers on page 128.*)

1. Say 'Have a beer'.   **2.** Say 'Have a sandwich'.   **3.** Say 'Have a coffee'.
4. Say 'Have an ice cream'.   **5.** Say 'Have an orangeade'.

Tip

To address members of your family, close friends and people with whom you are on first name terms, you use the informal **tu**, instead of the formal **Lei**, and the second person singular of the verb. The verb endings for **tu** are different from those for **Lei**. The ending for the present tense is **-i**: **hai, prendi**.

Many expressions relating to physical sensations use the verb **avere** ('to have'):

ho fame	ho sete	ho caldo	ho freddo	ho sonno

When the adjective **buono, buona** ('good') precedes the word to which it refers, it behaves like **uno, una**.

buon gelato	good ice cream	**buono studente**	good student
buon'idea	good idea	**buona brioche**	good bun

The plural is regular: **buoni, buone.**

Panorama italiano

Service areas on Italian motorways are very similar to those in other European countries. The largest ones include snack bars, restaurants and shops selling regional specialities. Food is usually of a high standard.

Travel

Going by taxi

Vocabolario

il taxi	taxi
la stazione	station
la stazione ferroviaria	railway station
accanto a	next to
la piazza	square
in arrivo	on its way
arrivi	arrivals
partenze	departures
vado (andare)	I go, I am going
di fronte a	opposite
il castello	castle
lo zoo	zoo

Dialoghi

Paul McPherson has arranged to meet a friend at the bar opposite the railway station. As it is late he rings up a taxi firm.

Taxi operator	Pronto, taxi Alabarda.
Paul McPherson	Pronto, vorrei un taxi per andare alla stazione.
Taxi operator	Il suo indirizzo per favore?
Paul McPherson	Via San Giorgio 24, accanto alla piazza.
Taxi operator	Il taxi numero 50 è in arrivo.
Paul McPherson	Grazie.
Taxi operator	Prego.

In the taxi.

Driver	Alla stazione?
Paul McPherson	Sì, per favore.
Driver	Arrivi o partenze?
Paul McPherson	No, vado al bar di fronte alla stazione.
Driver	Di fronte alla stazione ferroviaria?
Paul McPherson	Sì.
Driver	Ecco la stazione; il bar è lì di fronte, accanto alla banca.
Paul McPherson	Grazie, quant'è?
Driver	15.000 lire.
Paul McPherson	Ecco 15.000 lire e 1000 per Lei.
Driver	Grazie.
Paul McPherson	Prego.

Esercizi

1 Look at the destinations and complete the sentences. (*Answers on page 128.*)

A   B   C   D   E

A Vorrei andare ....
B Vorrei andare ....
C Vorrei andare ....
D Vorrei andare ....
E Vorrei andare ....

2   Comprehension. Listen to the recording and tick the correct boxes in the grid. (*Answers on page 128.*)

	di fronte	accanto	alla scuola	allo zoo	all'aeroporto	al castello
la stazione è						
il bar Neri è						
il pronto soccorso è						
la pizzeria è						
la banca è						

3   Use the visual prompts below to book a taxi, following the format of the first dialogue. (*Answers on page 128.*)

Tip

The verb **andare** ('to go') is irregular. The most useful forms are given on page 136.

In Italian addresses the house number follows the name of the street. The Italian equivalent of 10 Green Street would be **Via Verde 10**.

Note that **di fronte a** means 'opposite' and not 'in front of'.

Panorama italiano

Taxis can be found at taxi ranks or booked by phone. The wait is usually very brief. Taxis are identified by a number or a name.
On placards and maps the railway station is abbreviated to **stazione FS**. FS stands for **Ferrovie dello Stato** (State Railways).

Numbers

Weights and measurements

Vocabolario

un chilo (chili)	a kilo (kilos)
un litro	a litre
un metro	a metre
un centimetro	a centimetre
un chilometro (chilometri)	a kilometre (kilometres)
il miglio (le miglia)	mile (miles)
dista (distare)	is distant
quanto dista Roma da qua?	how far is Rome from here?
qua	here
metti (mettere)	you put (*informal*)
circa	about
caro, cara	expensive
la benzina	petrol
pesi (pesare)	you weigh (*informal*)
peso	I weigh
alto	tall
quanto sei alto?	how tall are you?
sei (essere)	you are (*informal*)

Dialoghi

Mrs Carpenter wants to go to Rome and asks her friend Carlo about the distance.

Mrs Carpenter	Carlo, quanto dista Roma da qua?
Carlo	Circa trenta chilometri.

Mrs Carpenter and her friend Carlo decide to drive to Rome. They stop for petrol.

Carlo	Sessantamila lire, per favore.
Mrs Carpenter	Quanti litri metti con sessantamila lire?
Carlo	Circa trenta litri.
Mrs Carpenter	È cara la benzina in Italia!

Two friends discuss their height and weight!

Marta	Quanto pesi?
Michele	Peso circa ottanta chili, e tu?
Marta	Cinquantadue chili, e quanto sei alto?
Michele	Uno e ottantasei, e tu?
Marta	Uno e sessantaquattro.

Discussing cars and mileage.

Federico	Quanti chilometri fa la tua auto con un litro?
Marcella	Circa sette.

Esercizi

1   Listen to the dialogues again. For each one write the correct measurement(s) under the picture. (*Answers on page 128.*) ∩

A   B

1 .... 2 .... 3 **A** height .... 4 ....
                                                weight ....
                                            B height ....
                                                weight ....

2   Match the English measurements with the Italian ones. (*Answers on page 128.*)
   A five miles   **1** mezzo chilo
   B eight kilos   **2** sessanta chilometri
   C half a kilo   **3** otto chili
   D sixty kilometres   **4** cinque miglia
   E one pound   **5** una libbra

3   Imagine you are Maria and answer the three questions on the recording. Use the prompts below and make complete sentences. (*Answers on page 128.*) ∩

   1. cinquantasei chili **2.** circa seicento chilometri **3.** un metro e sessantotto

Tip

Peso means 'I weigh' and **pesi** is the informal form (**tu**) 'you weigh'. They are both forms of the verb **pesare**.
Use **al, alla**, etc. to translate the English 'a' or 'per' used in measurements in this context.

duemila lire al chilo/al litro	2000 lire a kilo/a litre
tremila lire alla bottiglia	3000 lire a bottle
un milione al mese	1,000,000 per month

If you still prefer to use miles to express distance, note that (**il**) **miglio** ('mile') becomes (**le**) **miglia** in the plural.

Panorama italiano

Weights and measures
In Italy the metric system of weights and measures is well established. Instead of pounds and stones Italians always use kilos. A kilo is 2.2 lbs and a stone is 6.35 kgs; instead of miles Italians use kilometres. To convert kilometres into miles divide by 8 and multiply by 5, so 8 kilometres equals 5 miles. Instead of yards, feet and inches Italians use metres. One metre is 39.4 inches or 3.3 feet.

UNIT 25 Travel

Going by bus

Vocabolario

il centro	town centre
prendere	to take
l'autobus	bus
scendere	to get off
il porto	harbour
la fermata (dell'autobus)	(bus) stop
prima di	before
salire	to get on
bisogna	one has to
il biglietto	ticket
il giornalaio	newsagent
il blocchetto (di biglietti)	book (of tickets)
la stazione delle autocorriere	bus station
la pineta	pine wood
il duomo	main church

Dialoghi

Mr and Mrs Richmond decide to visit the town centre using public transport. They ask a passer-by for information.

Mrs Richmond	Scusi, per andare in centro?
Passer-by	Bisogna prendere l'autobus numero 1 e scendere al porto.
Mrs Richmond	Grazie, dov'è la fermata, per favore?
Passer-by	La fermata è lì di fronte, ma prima di salire bisogna comprare il biglietto dal giornalaio.

At the newsagent.

Mrs Richmond	Due biglietti per l'autobus, per favore.
Newsagent	Un biglietto costa 1100 lire, il blocchetto di sei biglietti costa 6600 lire e il blocchetto di dieci biglietti costa 10.000 lire.
Mrs Richmond	Allora vorrei un blocchetto di sei biglietti.

Esercizi

1 Which number? Look at the information on bus routes opposite and then match each picture to the correct route. You have not come across the word for one of these destinations before. Which one? (*Answers on page 128.*)

| **A** | **B** | **C** | **D** |

FERMATA AUTOBUS		FERMATA AUTOBUS	
1	Camping Pineta/Centro	24	Duomo/Stazione autocorriere
2	Stazione FS/Spiaggia	11	Pzza Garibaldi/Porto

2 Which bus? Listen to the recording. Six people want to go to different places. Look at the bus routes above and write in the grid which buses will take them to their destination. (*Answers on page 128.*)

Passenger	Bus	Passenger	Bus
A		D	
B		E	
C		F	

3 Now it's your turn to enquire about buses. Listen to the recording and follow the prompts below. You speak first. (*Answers on page 128.*)

1. Ask 'Excuse me, to go to the railway station?' **2.** Ask 'Where is the bus stop, please?' **3.** Ask 'Where can I buy a ticket?' **4.** Ask 'How much does a book of tickets cost?'

Tip

Generally the verb **andare** ('to go') takes **in** before the names of streets, squares and the word **centro**. In all other cases it takes **al, alla,** etc.: **al duomo, alla spiaggia.**

The verb **prendere** ('to catch') is used for all means of transport:
prendere il treno/l'autobus/l'aereo/un taxi

To say 'before doing something' use **prima di** + the infinitive form of the verb:

prima di salire	before getting on

in also combines with the definite article to produce a single word:

	il	lo	l'	i	gli	la	l'	le
in	**nel**	**nello**	**nell'**	**nei**	**negli**	**nella**	**nell'**	**nelle**

One way to express what one must do is to use the invariable verb **bisogna** followed by the infinitive:

bisogna prendere ... one needs to catch ...

Panorama italiano

Bus services in Italian towns are usually cheap and reliable. Tickets must be purchased in advance from selected bars and newsagents. Tickets are mechanically stamped on the bus. Although this is a simple operation, the written instructions given on the bus are difficult to understand. The verb **obliterare** (to cancel) is used for stamping. Follow what other passengers do. The cost of a ticket normally covers the whole route but you may need an extra ticket for bulky baggage.

Shopping

At the baker's

la panetteria	bakery
il pane	bread
un etto	100 grams
il biscotto (i biscotti)	biscuit (biscuits)
il frollino (i frollini)	shortbread biscuit (shortbread biscuits)
fresco, freschi	fresh
ancora caldi	still warm
un trancio	a slice
duemila al trancio	2000 lire a slice
altro?	anything else?
mi dà ...?	can you give me ...?
fanno ...	they come to ...
ne	of it/them
Quant'è in tutto?	How much is it in total?

 Dialogo

Mrs Mellini goes to the baker's.

Baker	Buongiorno, signora Mellini.
Signora Mellini	Buongiorno. Mi dà un chilo di pane?
Baker	Sì. Ecco un chilo di pane. Altro?
Signora Mellini	Mi dà un etto di biscotti. Cosa ha?
Baker	Allora, ho i frollini freschi, ancora caldi!
Signora Mellini	Bene, allora me ne dà due etti.
Baker	Sì, signora Mellini, altro?
Signora Mellini	Sì. Quanto costa la pizza?
Baker	2000 al trancio.
Signora Mellini	Ne prendo uno allora.
Baker	Altro?
Signora Mellini	No, basta grazie.
Baker	Allora 4000 il pane, i biscotti 3200, un trancio di pizza 2000. In tutto fanno ... 9200 lire.
Signora Mellini	Ecco a Lei.
Baker	Grazie e buongiorno.

Esercizi

 1 Le quantità giuste. Listen to the recording and write the quantity and price on the price tags. (*Answers on page 128.*)

A   B   C

2 Read the dialogue and fill in the missing words. (*Answers on page 128.*)

Signora Mellini	Buongiorno. Mi ...... un .... di pane?
Baker	Altro?
Signora Mellini	Sì, dei .... Che cosa ......?
Baker	.... questi frollini. Sono .... caldi.
Signora Mellini	E questa pizza, quanto costa?
Baker	2000 lire ...... trancio.

3 Ed ora la tua spesa. It is now your turn to go shopping at the baker's. To begin with, the baker asks what you would like. Listen to the recording and follow the prompts below. (*Answers on page 128.*)

1. Say you would like two kilos of bread.   **2.** Ask how much is the pizza?
3. Say 'I want two (slices) of it'.   **4.** Say 'Yes, do you have fresh biscuits?'
5. Say 'I would like 200 grams'.   **6.** Ask 'How much is it in total?'

Tip

Like **andare** (Unit 23), also **fare** ('to do', 'to make', 'to come to') and **dare** ('to give') are irregular **-are** verbs:

fanno	they do/make/come to	**danno**	they give

mi ('to me') is called an indirect object pronoun. In Italian it goes in front of the verb:

Mi dà un chilo di pane.   Can you give me a kilo of bread?

ne is used to replace a word or expression you have already mentioned and do not want to repeat. It goes in front of the verb:

Ne compro due.   I'll buy two of them.

Extra practice
Rewrite these sentences by substituting the underlined word(s) with the particle **ne**. (*Answers on page 128.*)

Vorrei tre <u>brioche</u>	**.......... vorrei tre.**
Marco compra due <u>pizze</u>	**Marco .... compra due.**
Prendo <u>un etto di biscotti</u>.	**.......... prendo uno.**
Quanti <u>figli</u> ha?	**.......... ho due.**

Panorama italiano

Bread is an important ingredient in the Italian diet. There are many kinds of bread, and recipes and names may vary according to the region and the local produce. **Pancarrè** looks like bread for toasting but does not taste the same as the English equivalent. Taste the different kinds of local breads.

UNIT 27 Leisure

Going to the cinema

Vocabolario

libero, libera	free
andiamo (andare)	we go, let's go, shall we go?
senti (sentire)	listen (*informal*)
stasera	tonight
volentieri	gladly
il cinema all'aperto	open-air cinema
sennò	if not, otherwise
ottimo, ottima	excellent
danno (dare)	they're showing
un giallo	thriller
la fantascienza	science fiction
adoro (adorare)	I love, I am mad about
passo (passare)	I'll come by
da me	to/at my house
da te	to/at your house
il ripasso	revision
noi	we

Dialogo

It is a warm summer evening, Emanuela rings up Simona.

Emanuela	Pronto, Simona, sono Emanuela, come va?
Simona	Bene, grazie e tu?
Emanuela	Bene. Sei libera stasera?
Simona	Sì, sono libera.
Emanuela	Senti, andiamo al cinema?
Simona	Volentieri. Fa molto caldo, andiamo a un cinema all'aperto?
Emanuela	Ottima idea, al Parco delle Rose danno un giallo, sennò all'Ariston c'è il festival del film di fantascienza!
Simona	Io adoro la fantascienza. A che ora comincia il film?
Emanuela	Alle 10.
Simona	Va bene! Passi da me?
Emanuela	Sì. Passo da te alle 9 e mezza.
Simona	Va bene, ciao.
Emanuela	Ciao.

Esercizi

1 Broken sentences. Match the two halves to make complete sentences. (*Answers on page 128.*)

A Marina e io   1 passa da Emanuela.
B Domenica Simona e io   2 va in Galles.
C Giovedì Emanuela   3 andiamo al cinema.
D Stasera Paul   4 andiamo da Marina.
E Come va?   5 Bene, grazie e tu?

2 Choosing a film. It is Thursday night and Simona is thinking of going to see a film. She rings up the local cinema and hears a recorded message. Listen to the recording and complete the grid below in English. Try to guess the English name of the film starring Matt Dillon. (*Answers on page 128.*)

Day	Film	Additional information
....	....	....
....	....	....
....	....	....
....	....	....
....	....	....
....	....	....

3 Invite a friend. Use the first three questions Emanuela asks in the dialogue on page 58 as a model to ask a friend if he or she would like to come out and go to an open-air pizzeria tonight. Write down your part of the conversation, then read it aloud. (*Answers on page 128.*)

Tip

The irregular verb **andare** ('to go') is used in many idiomatic expressions:

Come va?	How are you? *Literally* How is it going?
va bene	very well, that's fine

The Italian equivalent of 'we' is **noi** and the corresponding present tense ending of the verb is **-iamo**:

andiamo, passiamo, sentiamo.

Ripasso
tu is used in place of **Lei** when talking to family, friends and children. For all regular verbs ending with **-are, -ere, -ire** the second person singular (**tu** form) of the present tense ends in **-i**: **abiti, chiudi, apri**. See conjugation tables on page 135.

Panorama italiano

In Italian it is important to distinguish between formal and informal address. The informal **tu** is used only for family, friends and children. Don't use it until you have been invited to do so.

The evening performances at cinemas start late, around 8 p.m. with the last show around 10 p.m. Open-air cinema performances cannot start before dark.

Test yourself

Revision

1 Food and drink. Write in Italian the two missing words. It could be a word of opposite meaning (**sì/no**), an associated word (**cugino, zio**) or it could be in association with a grammatical rule (**è/sono**). (*Answers on page 128.*)

A ....
fame ....
freddo

B ....
mamma ....
salire

C ....
chiude ....
chiudono

2 Weights and measurements. Write in Italian the measurements mentioned on the recording. (*Answers on page 128.*)

A _____

B _____ _____

C _____

D _____

3 Fill in the gaps. Complete the dialogue with the missing words. (*Answers on page 128.*)

| va | chiusi | chiude | ristorante | apre | ha | pizzeria |

Gabriella ..... fame e ..... al supermercato. Il supermercato .... alle tre e mezza e .... alle nove. Di solito va al .... o alla .... per mangiare, ma oggi sono ....

4 Finding your way. Use the prompts below to answer the questions on the recording. To begin with you will be asked where the station is. (*Answers on page 128.*)

1. Say 'Opposite the castle'.
2. Say 'Next to the station'.
3. Say 'It's there, opposite, next to the castle'.

5 Match up the phrases and write down the first letters of the column on the right to obtain the name of a famous Italian square. (*Answers on page 128.*)

1 Scusi, questo autobus va in centro?   **a** Vorrei un biglietto per il centro.
2 Vorrei un'   **b** obliterare?
3 Desidera?   **c** Nove. L'autobus numero nove va in centro
4 Che cos'è   **d** aranciata.
5 Per il centro che numero devo prendere?   **e** No, va al porto.
6 Vorrei andare   **f** alla spiaggia.

6 Complete the crossword and you will find a famous Oscar-winning Italian film in the shaded column. (*Answers on page 128.*)

1	
2	
3	
4	
5	
6	
7	
8	
9	

Clues   **1.** Definite article in front of 'teatro' is ......
2. Adoro ...... fantascienza.   **3.** ...... da te alle nove
4. .... idea!   **5.** .... libera stasera, Simona?
6. Quant'è in ....?   **7.** L'Ariston è .... centro.
8. Quante brioche? .... vorrei tre (Italian used for 'of them').   **9.** A che .... comincia il film?

7 Shopping. Rearrange these words to make proper sentences.
(*Answers on page 128.*)

1 pane un di chilo dà mi?
2 la costa quanto pizza?
3 salire prima di, comprare biglietto il bisogna giornalaio dal

8 Practising verbs. Choose the correct verbs to complete these sentences.
(*Answers on page 128.*)

dà	vado	pesi	prendi	prendo	dista	ho	hai	vorrei	sei	è	è

.... fame, Giovanni? Sì, mamma, ... fame e sete. Che cosa .... da bere? Io .... una coca cola. Questa coca .... calda! .... un gelato! .... in vacanza. Quant' .... ? Cinquemila lire. Quanto .... Roma da Milano? Margherita, quanto .... alta? e quanto .... ? Mi .... un chilo di pane?

9 Hidden words. Find six words you have learned in Units 22–28. Consider all possibilities including diagonals. (*Answers on page 128.*)

X	Y	W	N	O	J	R	T	A	Z	A	C	L
T	R	A	N	C	I	O	Z	R	F	P	V	C
O	C	F	A	Z	L	N	B	R	C	I	N	Q
A	F	U	G	T	E	A	A	I	H	N	R	S
E	H	V	A	T	O	E	F	V	R	E	B	S
L	I	O	R	I	U	I	R	O	S	T	O	O
M	F	A	N	P	U	V	W	T	Y	A	X	L
N	P	C	H	I	L	O	M	E	T	R	O	N
R	B	I	S	C	O	T	T	I	P	Q	V	Z

Food and drink

At the restaurant

Vocabolario

As you are now familiar with the Italian pronunciation the vocabulary is not on the recording. Read it through and practise saying it out loud before going on to the dialogues.

siete (essere)	you are (*plural*)
in quanti siete?	how many are you?
avete (avere)	you have (*plural*)
prenotato (prenotare)	booked, reserved
il menu	menu
consigliare	to recommend
cosa ci consiglia?	what do you recommend to us?
cosa mi consiglia?	what do you recommend to me?
come primo	as first course
gli gnocchi	potato dumplings
il granchio	crab
la rucola	rocket
la specialità della casa	speciality of the house
il secondo	main course
il pesce	fish
gli scampi	scampi
alla griglia	grilled
sono molto buoni	are very good
la carne	meat
il fegato	liver
alla veneziana	Venetian style
da bere?	(what will you have) to drink?
il vino bianco	white wine
l'acqua minerale	mineral water
non gassata	still
al pomodoro	with tomato sauce
le melanzane	aubergines

Dialoghi

Mr and Mrs Richmond eat out at a restaurant in Venice.

Waitress	Buona sera, signori. In quanti siete?
Mr Richmond	Siamo in due.
Waitress	Avete prenotato?
Mr Richmond	Sì.
Waitress	Ecco un tavolo per due ed ecco il menu.
Mr Richmond	Grazie. Cosa ci consiglia come primo?
Waitress	Gli gnocchi con granchio e rucola sono una specialità della casa.
Mr Richmond	E cosa ci consiglia come secondo?
Waitress	Come pesce gli scampi alla griglia sono molto buoni, e come carne c'è il fegato alla veneziana.

Waitress	Da bere?
Mr Richmond	Mi consiglia il vino della casa?
Waitress	Sì, è molto buono.
Mr Richmond	Allora mezzo litro di vino bianco della casa.
Mrs Richmond	E una bottiglia d'acqua minerale non gassata.

Esercizi

1 Piatti italiani (Italian dishes). Match the pictures with the names of the dishes. (*Answers on page 128.*)

A   **B**   **C**   **D**   **E**   **F**

1 Spaghetti al pomodoro   **2** Scampi alla griglia   **3** Gnocchi   **4** Pizza alla rucola   **5** Risotto   **6** Bistecca alla fiorentina

2 In quanti siete? Listen to the waitress welcoming five groups of diners and write down how many people there are in each group. (*Answers on page 128.*)

A _____   **B** _____   **C** _____   **D** _____   **E** _____

3 Order a meal. You are in a restaurant in Florence with your friend Graham, who is a vegetarian. Read the menu below and say your orders in Italian for items 2 and 3 as first courses, 5 and 6 as main courses, ½ litre of white wine and mineral water. Which dishes did Graham choose? (*Answers on pages 128–29.*)

Primi piatti
1 Spaghetti al pomodoro
2 Gnocchi al pesto
3 Risotto di scampi

Secondi piatti
4 Bistecca alla fiorentina
5 Scampi alla griglia
6 Melanzane alla parmigiana

Tip

molto means 'very' as in 'very good'. When used like this **molto** does not change but the adjective that follows must agree with its subject, as in the following examples:

Il risotto è molto buono.	**La pizza è molto buona.**
Gli spaghetti sono molto buoni.	**Le melanzane sono molto buone.**

When you use the verb **consigliare** you need to express to whom the recommendation/advice is given. For 'to us' use **ci** and for 'to me' use **mi**. These pronouns are placed immediately before the verb:

Cosa ci consiglia?	What do you recommend (to us)?
Cosa mi consiglia?	What do you recommend (to me)?

The second person plural is normally used in both formal and informal situations:

In quanti siete?	How many of you are there?
Avete prenotato?	Have you booked?

Panorama italiano

a combined with the appropriate form of the article tells you how a dish is prepared:

alla griglia   grilled   **alla veneziana**   in Venetian style.

House wine is always sold in the following measures: ¼ litre, ½ litre and 1 litre.

 Leisure

Buying and renting on the beach

Vocabolario

la spiaggia	beach
l'ingresso	admission ticket, entrance
noleggiare	to rent, to hire
l'ombrellone	beach umbrella
il giorno	day
la sedia	chair
la sedia a sdraio	deck-chair
va bene	that's all right
a Lei	to you (formal)
dare	to give
da dare	to be given
il bagnino	beach attendant
l'abbonamento	season ticket
l'abbonamento stagionale	season ticket for the whole season

 ### Dialogo

At the beach entrance.

Cashier	Prego, desidera?
Mrs Bruce	Due ingressi alla spiaggia.
Cashier	Due ingressi sono 7800 lire.
Mrs Bruce	Desidero anche noleggiare un ombrellone e due sedie a sdraio.
Cashier	Per un giorno?
Mrs Bruce	Sì, per un giorno.
Cashier	L'ombrellone costa 4000 lire al giorno e una sedia a sdraio costa 2000 lire al giorno.
Mrs Bruce	Va bene.
Cashier	Allora due ingressi 7800 lire, due sedie a sdraio 4000 lire, un ombrellone 4000 lire: fa 15.800 lire in tutto.
Mrs Bruce	Ecco a Lei 50.000 lire.
Cashier	Ed ecco a Lei gli ingressi, i biglietti per l'ombrellone e le sedie a sdraio da dare al bagnino, e 34.200 lire di resto.
Mrs Bruce	Grazie, buongiorno.

Esercizi

1 A bit of maths. Mr and Mrs Bruce and their three children Alistair (9), Duncan (6) and Fiona (4) are going to spend a week on the beach in August. They want to rent a beach umbrella and two deck-chairs for the week. Study the price list opposite and find the best deal for them. (*Answers on page 129.*)

	dal 20.5	al 10.9
INGRESSO ALLA SPIAGGIA	adulti	bambini (6–12 anni)
Prezzo al giorno	3.900	1.500
Abbonamento di 10 ingressi	31.000	10.000
Abbonamento stagionale	150.000	70.000

	dall'11.9 al 19.5	dal 20.5 al 10.9
SEDIE A SDRAIO		
Al giorno	2.000	3.000
In abbonamento/al giorno (minimo 7 giorni)	1.000	2.500
OMBRELLONI		
Al giorno	4.000	8.500
In abbonamento/al giorno (minimo 7 giorni)	2.500	6.500

2 Matching. The grid below contains a list of holidaymakers and descriptions of their holidays. Listen to the recording twice and use the information given below to match the holidaymakers with their requests. (*Answers on page 129.*)

Holidaymaker	Type of Accommodation	Days
Ms Benson	Hotel Savoy	10
The Bruces	Camping Pineta	7
Signori Colombo	own holiday flat	all summer
Signora Campana and grandson	none	day excursion

3 Your requests. You have won a 10-day beach holiday in Italy. Use the visual prompts below to ask what you would like at the beach entrance. (*Answers on page 129.*)

A

B

C

Tip

The infinitive of Italian verbs can end in **-are, -ere** and **-ire**.
desiderare is a regular verb ending in **-are**. This means that it follows a predictable pattern, see the conjugation tables on page 135.

After a noun, the construction **da** + infinitive conveys the idea of something to be done:

| **un biglietto da dare al bagnino** | a ticket to be given to the beach attendant |
| **un film da vedere** | a film to be seen, a film not to be missed |

Verbs ending in **-ciare** and **-giare** drop the **-i-** before another **-i** or **-e**:

| **cominci** | you begin | **noleggiamo** | we rent |

Panorama italiano

Most Italian beaches are privately run and there is an entry fee. Consequently, they are clean and very well looked after, under the constant supervision of a life-guard (the **bagnino**). In Italian mythology **bagnini** are strikingly attractive and a national beauty contest is held every summer to find the most handsome.

31 Away from home

At the tourist information office

Vocabolario

desiderate? (desiderare)	can I help you?, what would you like?
cerchiamo (cercare)	we're looking for
cosa cercate?	what are you looking for?
trovate (trovare)	you will find
in macchina	by car
siete in macchina?	do you have a car?, are you travelling by car?
camminiamo (camminare)	we are walking
se camminate volentieri	if you are happy to walk
la zona	area
l'ufficio informazioni	information office
il monumento	monument
la fortezza	fortress
rinascimentale, rinascimentali	renaissance (adjective)
il centro sportivo	sports centre
i bagni termali	thermal/spa baths
la passeggiata	walk
il bosco	wood
nei boschi	in the woods
la villa	villa
il depliant	leaflet
la mappa	map
il sentiero	path
nel, nella, nei, nelle	in the

Dialogo

Two young backpackers go into the tourist office in Castelnuovo.

Assistant	Buongiorno, desiderate?
Tourist 1	Cerchiamo informazioni su questa zona.
Assistant	Siete in macchina?
Tourist 2	No, ma camminiamo volentieri.
Assistant	Qui c'è un po' di tutto. I monumenti sono: la fortezza rinascimentale e il duomo. Poi c'è il centro sportivo. Se camminate volentieri, a cinque chilometri da qui, a Terme, trovate i bagni termali e nei boschi ci sono ville rinascimentali.
Tourist 1	Ha una mappa, per favore?
Assistant	Ecco un depliant della zona e una mappa dei sentieri.
Tourist 2	Grazie.

Esercizi

1 Match the people in the drawings opposite with the places listed below. (*Answers on page 129.*)

    1 La fortezza, il duomo, le ville rinascimentali
    2 Il centro sportivo
    3 Le passeggiate nei boschi
    4 I bagni termali

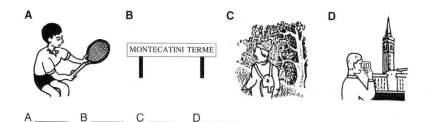

A   B   C   D

A _____ B _____ C _____ D _____

2   Finding your way. Listen to the recording. Four groups of people are asking for directions. Write down where each group wants to go. (*Answers on page 129.*)

A ....
B ....
C ....
D ....

3   At the tourist information office. Listen to the recording and ask for information using the prompts given below. The assistant begins by asking you what you want. (*Answers on page 129.*)

1. Say 'We are looking for information on this area'.   2. Say 'Yes, we have a car'   3. Say 'Do you have a map, please?'   4. Say 'Thank you'.

Tip

The present tense is used in Italian for actions happening at this moment, as well as for habitual actions (see Unit 46):

cerchiamo   we are looking for   **camminiamo**   we are walking

Verbs ending in **-care** or **-gare** add **-h** before the **tu** ending and the **noi** ending:

cercare   **(tu) cerchi**   **(noi) cerchiamo**
pagare   **(tu) paghi**   **(noi) paghiamo**

The **voi** form of the present tense ends in **-ate** for all **-are** verbs, **-ete** for all **-ere** verbs and **-ite** for all **-ire** verbs. Remember it is used in both formal and informal situations (Unit 29).

cercare (voi) cercate   **prendere (voi) prendete**   **partire (voi) partite**

Adjectives ending in **-e** have two forms only, **-e** for the singular and **-i** for the plural.

	Singular	Plural
Masc	**monumento rinascimentale**	**monumenti rinascimentali**
Fem	**villa rinascimentale**	**ville rinascimentali**

Panorama italiano

The word **gabinetti** (toilets) is found on public toilets but euphemisms are used in speech and in most private establishments. The most common are **bagno** (bathroom) and the French word **toilette**.

Away from home

Understanding and giving directions

Vocabolario

il commissariato di polizia	police station
la cattedrale	cathedral
l'albergo	hotel
non lo so	I don't know (it)
a destra	on/to the right
sulla destra	on the right
a sinistra	on/to the left
sempre dritto	straight on
in fondo a	at the end of
in fondo a destra	at the end on the right
all'incrocio	at the crossroads
al semaforo	at the traffic lights
tra	between
proprio qui	right here

Dialoghi

Mr Bullock asks his friend for directions. He needs to find out where the station and the cathedral are.

Mr Bullock Scusa, dov'è la cattedrale?
Friend Mi dispiace, non lo so.

Mr Bullock asks a passer-by.

Mr Bullock Scusi, per andare alla cattedrale?
Passer-by Allora. La cattedrale … Deve andare sempre dritto e poi la prima a destra. La cattedrale è in fondo alla strada.
Mr Bullock E la stazione è lontana dalla cattedrale?
Passer-by No, è vicina. È nella strada dietro la cattedrale, a sinistra.

Mr Bullock then asks for the police station.

Mr Bullock Scusi, dov'è il commissariato di polizia?
Passer-by All'incrocio va a sinistra. Poi al semaforo gira a destra. Il commissariato di polizia è davanti alla banca.
Mr Bullock Grazie.
Passer-by Prego.

Mr Bullock asks his friend for the Albergo Carinni.

Mr Bullock Scusa, dov'è l'albergo Carinni?
Friend Allora, in fondo a destra, al semaforo ancora a destra. A 500 metri sulla sinistra vicino alla pizzeria.

Esercizi

1 A treasure has been hidden in one of the buildings on the map. Where is it? Follow the instructions on the recording. (*Answers on page 129.*)

| 1 Banca |
| 2 Farmacia |
| 3 Lattaio |
| 4 Fermata |
| 5 Museo |

FERMATA

You are here

2 A friend sends you directions for getting to her house. Translate them into English. (*Answers on page 129.*)

> *La mia casa è vicino alla stazione. Dalla stazione prendi la prima strada a destra, la seconda a sinistra e dopo il secondo semaforo gira a destra. Non è lontano. Circa mezzo chilometro. Io abito nel palazzo dietro la farmacia.*

3 Somebody stops you and asks for information. Listen to the recording and try to help using the prompts below. (*Answers on page 129.*)

1. Say 'I don't know, I am not from here'. **2.** Say 'It is straight on, the first on the left.' **3.** Say 'No, it is right here behind the cathedral.'

Tip

scusa is the informal way of saying 'excuse me'. If you stop a stranger, use the formal **scusi**.

Panorama italiano

The life of pedestrians!
Most Italian cities have kept their cobbled streets. Walking or cycling in the city centre can be quite difficult because of the high level of motorized traffic and because the narrow streets characteristic of most city centres do not always have pavements.
Traffic lights, in many areas of Italy, tend to be regarded as an option and pedestrian crossings are largely ignored. Be careful when you are crossing: look first left and then right.

Health

At the chemist's

Vocabolario

qualcosa	something
il mal di ...	... ache
lo stomaco	stomach
la testa	head
la gola	throat
la pastiglia	tablet
lo sciroppo	syrup
la ricetta	prescription
pieno, piena	full
volta (volte)	time (times)
dopo	after
il pasto	meal
il cucchiaio	spoon, spoonful
il flacone	bottle (*for medicines, cosmetics*)
Le	to you/you
deve	you must
consiglio (consigliare)	I advise
prendere	to take
deve prenderne ...	you need to take ... of it/them
che cosa?	what?
eccolo	here it is (*for a masculine noun*)
eccola	here it is (*for a feminine noun*)

Dialoghi

Mr Ghiotti has got a bad stomachache and headache. He goes to the chemist's and asks for some medicine.

Signor Ghiotti	Buongiorno. Ha qualcosa per il mal di testa e per il mal di stomaco?
Chemist	È per Lei?
Signor Ghiotti	Sì.
Chemist	Le consiglio queste pastiglie. Deve prenderne una prima dei pasti, tre volte al giorno.

Signor Ghiotti	Ha qualcosa per il mal di gola?
Chemist	Le consiglio questo sciroppo. Deve prenderne due cucchiai dopo i pasti.

Mrs Vecchioni goes to the doctor and asks for a particular brand of medicine for stomachache.

Signora Vecchioni	Vorrei un flacone di Cavoltrin.
Chemist	Ha la ricetta del medico?
Signora Vecchioni	Sì, eccola.
Chemist	Sono 3500 lire.

Esercizi

1 Listen to the recording and write in English what these people are suffering from. (*Answers on page 129.*)

A .... **B** .... **C** ....

2 Che cosa, quando e quanto? Read the instructions for taking this medicine and answer the following questions in English. (*Answers on page 129.*)

A What is it for?
B When should you take it?
C How much should you take?
D Is it suitable for babies?

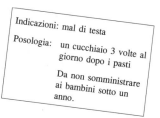

Indicazioni: mal di testa

Posologia: un cucchiaio 3 volte al giorno dopo i pasti

Da non somministrare ai bambini sotto un anno.

3 You have a bad headache and sore throat and go to the chemist's to buy some medicine. Follow the prompts below. The chemist begins by asking what you would like. (*Answers on page 129.*)

1. Ask 'Have you got anything for a headache and a sore throat?' **2.** Say 'Thank you. How much do I take per day?' **3.** Say 'No, thank you. How much is it?'

Tip

The present tense of **dovere** ('must', 'have to') is irregular, e.g. **devo, deve**.

Le translates 'to you' in the polite form. It is written with a capital.

When the verb accompanying **ne** ('of it', 'of them') is in the infinitive, you add **-ne** to the infinitive after dropping the final **-e**:

prendere	to take	**prenderne**	to take ... of it/them
mangiare	to eat	**mangiarne**	to eat ... of it/them

Panorama italiano

In Italy everyone has to choose their GP, for children this is a pediatrician. The GP deals with very general problems and often refers the patient to a specialist or to the hospital for more specific health problems. To go to a specialist you need to make an appointment and produce a request from your doctor. You can also go privately, in which case you don't need a medical request though you will have to pay the full fee. This tends to be very high. Pharmacists are very highly regarded and Italians very often ask for advice from their local pharmacist before consulting their doctor.

Information

Weather reports

il tempo	weather
bel tempo	good weather
brutto tempo	bad weather
che tempo fa?	what is the weather like?
le previsioni del tempo	weather forecast
piove	it rains, it is raining
sereno	clear
variabile	changeable
nuvoloso	cloudy
caldo	hot
freddo	cold
calmo	calm
mosso	rough
la temperatura	temperature
il sole	sun
la nuvola	cloud
la pioggia	rain
il temporale	storm
gradi	degrees
il cielo	sky
fino a	up to
da te	where you are
che ...?	what ...?/what kind of ...?

 Dialogo

Lorena is studying abroad. She rings her mum and asks what the weather is like in Bergamo.

Signora Mazza	Pronto, chi parla?
Lorena	Mamma, sono Lorena. Che tempo fa lì a Bergamo?
Signora Mazza	C'è il sole e fa molto caldo. Ci sono 36 gradi. E da te, che tempo fa?
Lorena	È nuvoloso, piove e fa freddo.
Signora Mazza	Che cosa fai questo weekend?
Lorena	Con questo brutto tempo resto a casa a studiare.

Carla and Roberto want to go sailing at the weekend and they are listening to the weather forecast on the radio, which mentions sailing conditions.

Announcer	Previsioni del tempo per oggi. Tempo variabile al Nord con piogge e temporali. Al Centro e al Sud, tempo sereno e caldo con temperature fino a 30 gradi al Sud. Mari: Tirreno e Ionio poco mossi; Adriatico calmo.

1 Weather reports. Listen to the recording and match each picture with the correct weather forecast. (*Answers on page 129.*)

A   **B**   **C**   **D**

1 _____   **2** _____   **3** _____   **4** _____

2 A call from Italy. Your Italian friend Elisabetta leaves a message on your answerphone, but some words aren't clear. Fill in the gaps with the words below. (*Answers on page 129.*)

| nuvola | molto caldo | calmo | sole | bel | sereno | buone | gradi |

Oggi fa .... tempo, c'è il .... e fa ....! Ci sono 38 ....! Il cielo è .... e non c'è una .... Il mare oggi è .... e posso nuotare bene. Le previsioni per domani sono ....

3 Now ring back your friend Elisabetta and check on the weather with her. You begin the conversation. Listen to the recording and use the prompts provided below. (*Answers on page 129.*)

1. Say 'Hello' and your name and ask 'Who is speaking please?'   **2.** Say 'Hello, Elisabetta, what is the weather like in Venice?'   **3.** Ask 'And is the sea calm? '   **4.** Ask 'And the forecast for tomorrow?'

Tip

chi? ('who?', 'whom?') is an invariable pronoun used only for people:

| **Chi parla?** | Who is speaking? |

che?, che cosa? is an invariable pronoun used only for things:

| **Che cosa fai?** | What are you doing? |
| **Che bevi?** | What are you drinking? |

che? ('what ...?', 'what kind of ...?') is an invariable adjective:

| **Che tempo fa?** | What is the weather like? |
| **Lei, che lavoro fa?** | What kind of work do you do? |

Panorama italiano

The weather plays an important role in Italian life and culture. Italians spend a great part of the year out of doors, especially in the South.
In summer, many theatrical performances, concerts and even fashion shows take place outside, taking advantage of the beauty of Italian squares.

Test yourself

Revision

1 Al ristorante. Match the waiter's sentences on the left with the customer's responses on the right to reconstruct the dialogue. (*Answers on page 129.*)

1 Buonasera, signori. Siete in due?
2 E da bere?
3 Gli scampi alla griglia.
4 Sì, ecco il tavolo ed ecco il menu.
5 Sì. E come secondo?
6 Gli spaghetti alla rucola sono ottimi!
7 Mezzo litro di vino bianco va bene?

A Cosa ci consiglia come pesce?
B Grazie. Allora ... che cosa ci consiglia per primo?
C Alla rucola? Sono la specialità della casa?
D Sì, c'è un tavolo per due?
E Va bene. Scampi per due.
F Una bottiglia di acqua minerale e il vino della casa.
G Benissimo.

2 Touring around. Listen to the recording and arrange the places listed below in the order you hear them. (*Answers on page 129.*)

☐ **A** la casa di Giulietta
☐ **B** i bagni termali
☐ **C** l'Arena
☐ **D** il duomo
☐ **E** le Terme di Sirmione
☐ **F** il castello
☐ **G** le ville del Palladio

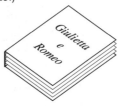

Giulietta e Romeo

3 Asking for directions. You are now in Verona. Ask the way to Juliet's house using the following prompts. You speak first. (*Answers on page 129.*)

1. Say 'Excuse me, to go to Juliet's house?' **2.** Say 'Straight on and then the second right and at the end left'. **3.** Ask 'Is it far from here?'

4 Illnesses. Look at these two people and write down their symptoms in Italian. (*Answers on page 129.*)

1    **2**

5 Expecting visitors. You are working in Italy and some English friends are visiting you. You know that they are keen to sample the local cuisine but they don't eat meat. You find the following ads for restaurants in the yellow pages. Select the most appropriate. (*Answers on page 129.*)

Mamma Rosa
Paninoteca
Gelateria

La Grande Muraglia -
Ristorante cinese

Da Bruno
specialità pesce

SELF-SERVICE
Ai due leoni:
Spaghetteria

6 Grammar practice. On a separate sheet of paper, group the following words according to their article **il, la, lo, l'**. (*Answers on page 129.*)

ingresso	sedia	bagnino	zoo	zio
cugino	ombrellone	cinema	spiaggia	amica
ristorante	secondo	carne	pesce	ufficio informazioni
stazione	albergo	taxi	stomaco	sciroppo

7 On a separate sheet of paper, group the verbs below under the correct person. (One verb goes under two columns.) (*Answers on page 129.*)

io (I)   **tu** (you familiar)   **Lei** (you formal)   **noi** (we)   **voi** (you plural)   **loro** (they)
          lei (she)
          lui (he)

sei	ha	dista	ho	prendi	consiglia
hai	prendo	vado	va	andiamo	metti
è	fanno	desidera	vorrei	comincia	passo
fa	desiderate	siete	sono	camminiamo

8 Weather forecast. Match each picture with the appropriate forecast. (*Answers on page 129.*)

A   **B**   **C**

1 Il cielo è sereno.   2 È nuvoloso con possibilità di piogge e temporali.
3 I mari sono mossi.

9 More weather forecasts. Listen to the weather forecast and decide which of these three plans you should go ahead with. (*Answers on page 129.*)

A go to the beach, **B** go for a pleasure cruise, **C** stay indoors and wrap up warm.

10 The maze. Your friend Paolo has lost his glasses and he needs to be directed out of the maze to the station. (*Answers on page 129.*)

stazione

Paolo

Shopping

At the post office

Vocabolario

il pacco (i pacchi)	packet (packets)
l'ufficio postale	post office
quei, quelle, quegli	those
quel, quell', quello, quella	that
spedisce (spedire)	you send by mail
parenti	relatives
pensare	to think
le feste	celebrations, feasts
in anticipo	early, in advance
metta (mettere)	put
la bilancia	scales
un quintale	a ton, *literally* kg 100
via aerea	air mail
via mare	surface mail
la raccomandata	recorded delivery letter
il francobollo	stamp
altro, altra, altri, altre	other
lo sportello	counter
la fila	queue
lunghissima	very long
l'oggetto	object
l'armadio	wardrobe, cupboard

Dialoghi

Mrs Bianco meets Mr Colombo, who is laden with lots of parcels.

Signora Bianco	Buongiorno, signor Colombo, dove va con tutti quei pacchi?
Signor Colombo	Buongiorno, signora Bianco, vado all'ufficio postale, sono regali di Natale per i nostri nipoti in America.
Signora Bianco	Spedisce già i regali di Natale?
Signor Colombo	Eh sì, quando i parenti sono lontani bisogna pensare alle feste in anticipo.

At the post office counter.

Assistant	Metta quel pacco sulla bilancia, per favore.
Signor Colombo	Questo non pesa molto, ma quell'altro pesa un quintale.
Assistant	Via aerea o via mare?
Signor Colombo	Via mare, grazie. Vorrei anche spedire una raccomandata e vedere quei nuovi francobolli.
Assistant	La raccomandata va bene ma per i francobolli speciali bisogna andare a quell'altro sportello.
Signor Colombo	Quello sportello lì? Con quella fila lunghissima? Ritorno un altro giorno!

Esercizi

1 Match the forms of 'that' and 'those' with the nouns. (*Answers on page 129.*)

| quell' | quello | quel | quella | quella | quelle | quegli | quei |

| raccomandata | bilancia | ufficio | francobolli | pacco |

| sportello | feste | oggetti |

2 Match the pictures with the sentences (*Answers on page 129.*)

A   B   C   D   E

1. Bisogna spedire quella lettera.   **4.** Bisogna pesare quel pacco.
2. Non bisogna fumare.   **5.** Non bisogna gettare oggetti.
3. Bisogna comprare i francobolli.

3 Write a sentence to say how much each of the following items weighs, using the appropriate form of **quel**. The first one has been done for you. (*Answers on page 129.*)

1 Quella valigia pesa 20 chili.

2 ....

3 ....

4 ....

5 ....

Tip

When the Italian words for 'that' and 'those' come before the nouns to which they refer, their endings are similar to those of the article **il**, **la**, etc.:

1. que*l* pacco	2. que*i* pacchi	3. quel*l'*armadio	4. que*gli* armadi
5. quel*la* lettera	6. quel*le* lettere	7. quel*l'*insalata	8. quel*le* insalate
9. quel*lo* zio	10. que*gli* zii		

Panorama italiano

The Italian postal service is very unreliable. Letters from abroad frequently take less time to reach Italian destinations than those sent between Italian cities. Fax transmission and electronic mail are therefore used extensively.

Vocabolario

vorremmo (volere)	we would like
volete (volere)	you wish
in treno	by train
arrivare	to arrive
l'arena	open-air theatre
l'espresso	express train
la coincidenza	connection
cambiare	to change
il rapido	intercity
l'unico	the only one
viaggia (viaggiare)	he/she/it travels
in orario	on time
devo pensarci	I need to think about it
parla (parlare)	you speak (*formal singular*)
parla italiano?	do you speak Italian?
vuole (volere)	you wish (*formal singular*)
ferma (fermare)	it stops

Dialogo

At the travel agent's in Cervignano.

Travel agent	Buongiorno. Prego desidera?
Mr Richmond	Buongiorno. Mia moglie ed io vorremmo andare in treno a Verona il 7 agosto.
Travel agent	A che ora volete arrivare?
Mr Richmond	Abbiamo biglietti per l'opera all'Arena, ma vorremmo arrivare nel pomeriggio e vedere la città.
Travel agent	C'è un espresso da Cervignano a Mestre alle 14:51. Arriva a Mestre alle 16:07 con coincidenza per Verona alle 16:17. Arriva a Verona alle 17:28.
Mr Richmond	Solo 10 minuti per cambiare! E se il treno ha ritardo?
Travel agent	Di solito questo treno viaggia in orario.
Mr Richmond	Bisogna sempre cambiare a Mestre? Non c'è un rapido?
Travel agent	No, questo è l'unico treno a quest'ora.
Mr Richmond	Devo pensarci, molte grazie.
Travel agent	Prego, buongiorno.

Esercizi

1 Scrambled sentences. The sentences in the following conversation are mixed up. Rearrange them in the correct order for the dialogue between Mr Cantoni and his travel agent. *(Answers on page 129.)*

   A Sì, bisogna cambiare treno e anche stazione due volte: a Parigi e a Londra.
   B In questa stagione non ci sono voli diretti da Verona a Manchester.

C   Grazie a Lei, buongiorno.
D   Dove esattamente?
E   Grazie, devo pensarci.
F   Vorrei andare in Inghilterra.
G   Veramente, vorrei andare in treno.
H   A Manchester.
I   Bisogna cambiare treno?
J   Allora deve prendere il treno per Parigi e da Parigi il treno per Londra e poi da Londra il treno per Manchester.

2   Station announcements. You are at the railway station in Cervignano and you have a second-class ticket to Milan. Listen to the announcements on the recording and answer the following question in English. *(Answers on page 129.)*

A   At which platform is the train?
B   Where should passengers for Florence go?
C   Why will passengers for Trieste be annoyed?
D   What type of ticket do you need to travel on the Romolo?

3   Giving travel information. An Italian client comes to your travel agency in Hull to find out about trains to Sheffield. Consult the timetable below, then listen to the recording and follow the prompts below. The client starts the conversation. *(Answers on page 129.)*

1. Say 'Yes, I speak Italian.'   2. Ask 'At what time do you want to arrive?'
3. Say 'Then there is only one train'.   4. Say 'It leaves Hull at 7.36 and arrives in Sheffield at 9.33'.   5. Say 'No, it is a through train'.

HULL	6.40	7.36	8.48
DONCASTER	7.44	8.41	9.46
SHEFFIELD	8.31	9.33	10.28

Tip

ci has a range of different meanings. In the expressions **pensare a** + noun ('to think about someone or something') and **credere a** + noun ('to believe in someone or something') **ci** can replace **a** + noun:

Pensi alle vacanze?	Are you thinking about the holidays?
Sì, ci penso.	Yes, I am thinking about them.

When **pensare** and **credere** appear in the infinitive form, the final **-e** is dropped and **ci** combines with the infinitive:

Voglio crederci.	I want to believe in it.
Devo pensarci.	I must think about it, I'll have to think about it

vuole 'you want' (singular) and **volete** 'you want' (plural) are forms of the verb **volere**, which is very irregular. You will find other forms on page 136.
vorremmo ('we would like') is the first plural of the conditional present. The singular is **vorrei** ('I would like').

Panorama italiano

Italian trains are considerably less expensive than in Great Britain; this is especially true of those labelled **diretto, espresso, locale**. For many fast trains (**rapido** and **Intercity**) a booking is required and you also have to pay an additional surcharge (**supplemento rapido**). This is a flat rate and makes **rapidi** uneconomical for short distances. Note that before getting on a train you need to validate your ticket (**obliterare il biglietto**) in a special machine placed on the platform. If you don't, you are liable to pay a very heavy fine.

Shopping

Buying fruit and vegetables at the market

Vocabolario

un ciuffo	a head
la mela	apple
la pesca (le pesche)	peach (peaches)
la ciliegia (le ciliege)	cherry (cherries)
l'albicocca (le albicocche)	apricot (apricots)
l'uva	grapes
il fico (i fichi)	fig (figs)
l'anguria	watermelon
l'insalata	salad
il pomodoro	tomato
il peperone	pepper
la cassetta	crate
troppo	too much
vanno bene	they are OK
vengono	they come, they cost
viene	it comes, it costs
capisco (capire)	I understand
spedisci (spedire)	you send
finisce (finire)	he/she/it finishes
preferiscono (preferire)	they prefer

Dialoghi

Mrs Mellini is doing her shopping at a fruit and vegetable market.

Signora Mellini	Buongiorno. Mi dà un chilo di mele, per favore.
Greengrocer	Ecco le mele. Altro?
Signora Mellini	Un chilo e mezzo di pesche.
Greengrocer	Serve altro?
Signora Mellini	Due chili di ciliege e uno di albicocche.
Greengrocer	Preferisce queste o quelle?
Signora Mellini	Vanno bene queste. Poi mi dà un ciuffo di insalata e mezzo chilo di pomodori.
Greengrocer	Ecco. Altro?
Signora Mellini	Sì, mi dà questi due peperoni; e quant'è questa anguria?
Greengrocer	Le angurie vengono 400 lire al chilo. Questa pesa 5 chili e 300. Allora facciamo 2000. Basta così?
Signora Mellini	Sì, basta così, grazie.

Walking among the stalls she notices some lovely grapes and decides to buy a few kilos.

Signora Mellini	Vorrei dell'uva bianca. Quanto viene questa?
Greengrocer	2500 lire al chilo o 10.000 lire la cassetta di 5 chili.
Signora Mellini	Me ne dà una cassetta allora. E questi fichi quanto vengono?
Greengrocer	4500 lire al chilo.
Signora Mellini	No, è troppo! Basta così.

Esercizi

1 The odd one out. (*Answers on page 129.*)
Which of these cannot be bought in kilos?

| mele | uva bianca | pane | benzina |

Which of these cannot be bought in different colours?

| albicocche | insalata | uva | peperoni |

Which of these cannot be used in fruit salad?

| albicocche | mele | pesche | pesce |

2 Mrs Mellini asks you to do her shopping. Listen to the recording and write down her shopping list in Italian. (*Answers on pages 129–30.*)

La spesa

3 Complete the dialogue at the greengrocer's. Listen to the recording and follow the prompts below. *(Answers on page 130.)*

1. Say 'I would like 2 ½ kilos of apples'.   **2.** Say 'I would like a kilo of grapes'.
3. Say 'White, please'.   **4.** Ask 'How much are the red peppers?'

Tip

Many verbs ending in **-ire** follow the pattern below:

prefer*isc*o	preferiamo
prefer*isc*i	preferite
prefer*isc*e	prefer*isc*ono

The pronunciation of **-sc** depends on the vowel following it: before **-o-** it is pronounced like 'sk-' as in 'sky'; before **-i** and **-e** it is pronounced like 'sh-' in 'shy'.

The forms **viene** ('he/she/it comes') and **vengono** ('they come') are used to express 'it costs' and 'they cost':

Viene/vengono 10.000 lire al chilo.   It costs/they cost 10,000 lire a kilo.

Extra practice
Insert the correct form of the verb in the following sentences. (*Answers on page 130.*)

1 Scusi, non .... (io – capire).
2 .... (tu – preferire) le pesche o le albicocche?
3 Marta e Marco .... (preferire) le ciliege.

Panorama italiano

In Italy fruit and vegetable markets are found in all urban centres. They are very colourful and offer a rich selection of fresh produce at a good price. Don't forget to try for a **sconto** ('discount'). In some places it is still an important part of the negotiation.

39 People

Describing people

Vocabolario

tuo, tua, tuoi, tue	your
mio, mia, miei, mie	my
quello, quella	that one
quelli, quelle	those ones
biondo, bionda	fair-haired
bruno, bruna	dark-haired
i capelli	hair
capelli lisci	straight hair
capelli ricci	curly hair
capelli bruni	dark hair
gli occhi	eyes
azzurro, azzurra	light blue
alto, alta	tall
piccolo, piccola	small, petite
grasso, grassa	fat, plump
magro, magra	slim
il ragazzo	boy
lungo, lunga, lunghi, lunghe	long
corto, corta, corti, corte	short
in gamba	bright, smart, with-it
simpatico, simpatica, simpatici, simpatiche	pleasant
sembrano (sembrare)	they look, seem
che	who/whom/which/that

Dialogo

Gabrio has recently started a new school. His mother has gone to pick him up.

Mother Allora, Gabrio, come va con la tua scuola?

Gabrio Bene, ho molti amici e i miei insegnanti sono in gamba. Ecco là la mia insegnante di inglese.

Mother Quella che parla con la signora Anita?

Gabrio No, la signora bionda nella Panda. E ecco i miei amici Giacomo e Stefano.

Mother Quelli che escono adesso?

Gabrio Sì, quello alto e magro è Giacomo e il ragazzo bruno con lui è Stefano.

Mother Il ragazzo un po' grasso?

Gabrio No, quello con i capelli corti e gli occhi azzurri. Il ragazzo un po' grasso è Matteo.

Mother Sembrano simpatici.

Gabrio Sì, sono simpatici e anche Luciana, quella bionda lì dietro, è simpatica ed è mia amica.

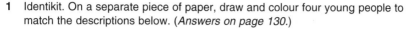

Esercizi

1 Identikit. On a separate piece of paper, draw and colour four young people to match the descriptions below. (*Answers on page 130.*)

A Gabrio è biondo e magro, ha i capelli lunghi e lisci e gli occhi azzurri.
B Martina è bruna e piccola, ha i capelli ricci.
C Stefano è bruno, alto e magro, ha i capelli corti e gli occhi azzurri.
D Luciana ha i capelli biondi e lisci, è piccola e un po' grassa.

2 Who is who? Listen to the recording and match the following characters with their descriptions. (*Answers on page 130.*)

A Princess Diana **B** Luciano Pavarotti **C** Charlie Chaplin **D** Mother Theresa

3 Oral practice. A friend meets you outside the office where you are working in Italy. Listen to the recording and use the prompts below to describe your friends to her. She speaks first. (*Answers on page 130.*)

1. Say 'Well, thank you. That is my friend Luisa'. **2.** Say 'The small slim one with straight brown hair'; then add 'And there are my friends Stefano and Giorgio.' **3.** Say 'The tall plump one with curly hair is Stefano'. **4.** Say 'He is the tall slim one, with long straight fair hair'. **5.** Say 'Yes, and he is also very pleasant'.

Tip

With the **tu** form of address the words for 'your' (possessives) are **tuo, tua** in the singular and **tuoi, tue** in the plural. Remember that the Italian words for 'your' must agree with the noun that follows:

il tuo amico	your friend (m)	**i tuoi amici**	your friends (m)
la tua insegnante	your teacher (f)	**le tue insegnanti**	your teachers (f)

che means 'who'/'whom'/'which' and 'that'. It is used to refer to both people and things:

i ragazzi che escono	the boys who are coming out
il libro che preferisco	the book I like best

When adjectives end in **-co** and **-go** in the singular, you usually insert an **-h-** before the plural endings to keep the sound. However, there are exceptions:

Singular	*Plural*		*Singular*	*Plural*
lungo	**lunghi**	*Exception* ⟶	**simpatico**	**simpatici**
lunga	**lunghe**		**simpatica**	**simpatiche**

Panorama italiano

Remember that the perception of physical attributes varies from country to country. This applies to height and size as well as to hair colour. Italians will describe as **biondo** or **bionda** people you may consider quite dark.

Information

Recognising colours, smells and flavours

Vocabolario

il colore	colour
bianco	white
nero	black
rosso	red
verde	green
giallo	yellow
blu	blue
rosa	pink
arancio	orange
amaro, amara	bitter
dolce	sweet
salato, salata	salty
piccante	spicy
saporito, saporita	tasty
secco, secca	dry
forte	strong, intense
l'ambiente	environment
l'arrosto	roast
il partito	(political) party
la bandiera	flag
perché	because
un po'	a bit
che colore preferisci?	what/which colour do you prefer/like best?

Dialoghi

Marta and Giovanni are discussing their favourite colours.

Marta   Il rosso è il mio colore preferito.
Giovanni   Io preferisco il verde perché è il colore del partito dell'ambiente: i Verdi.

Giuseppe and Gloria discuss flavours.

Gloria   Come ti sembra questo arrosto?
Giuseppe   Molto saporito ed anche un po' piccante.
Gloria   A me non piace; mi sembra un po' secco ed anche amaro.

Later on.

Gloria   Come prendi il caffè: dolce o amaro?
Giuseppe   Forte e amaro, prego.

Esercizi

1   Listen to the recording and write down in Italian the colour(s) mentioned in each phrase. Then match them with the translations on the right. (*Answers on page 130.*)

1 .... **A** the colours of the Italian flag are white, red and green
2 .... **B** in the blue sky

3 .... **C** yellow like a lemon
4 .... **D** white or red wine?
5 .... **E** as white as snow

2 Complete the crossword. You will find the Italian for 'violet' in the shaded column. (*Answers on page 130.*)

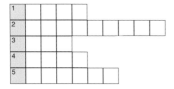

Clues **1** the third colour of the Italian flag **2** to meet **3** after **sette**
4 produced by cows **5** red + yellow =

3 Role plays. Listen to the three recordings and follow the prompts below. (*Answers on page 130.*)

A In a clothes shop. The sales assistant begins by asking what colour you prefer. **1.** Say 'I like the red one best'. **2.** Say 'No, thank you'.

B In the restaurant. You begin by asking the waiter what he recommends. **1.** Ask 'What do you recommend?' **2.** Say 'I prefer spicy things'.

C Coffee at friends. Your friend begins by asking how you like your coffee. **1.** Say 'Strong and sweet, please.'

Tip

Colours are adjectives and therefore agree in gender and number with the noun they accompany:

	Singular	Plural
Masc.	**un libro giallo**	**due libri gialli**
Fem	**una valigia gialla**	**due valige gialle**

Colours that end in **-e** like **verde** do not change in the feminine singular, and take **-i** in both masculine and feminine plural:

un giardino verd*e*	**due giardini verd*i***
una bandiera verd*e*	**due bandiere verd*i***

Colours that take their name from a particular object, like **rosa** ('pink') from **una rosa** ('a rose'), or which are foreign in origin, like **blu**, are invariable:

una cadillac ros*a*	**due cadillac ros*a***

Panorama italiano

Italy is a very colourful country in its food, its fashion, its people. Colours are used to express feelings or people's situations, e.g. **essere al verde** means 'to be hard up/poor', while **essere nero** means 'to be in a bad mood'.

Shopping

Buying clothes and shoes

Vocabolario

la gonna	skirt
la vetrina	shop-window
il camerino	changing room
la taglia	size (*for garments*)
il profumo	perfume
le scarpe	shoes
la camicetta	blouse
il numero	size (*for shoes*)
scozzese	tartan-pattern
da uomo	for men
di pelle	(*made of*) leather
sportivo	casual
marrone	brown
provare	to try on
mi piace	I like it
mi piacciono	I like them
piacere	to like
mi sta bene (stare)	it suits me

Dialoghi

Mary goes into a boutique to try on a skirt she's seen in the window.

Mary   Buongiorno, vorrei provare quella gonna scozzese che avete in vetrina.
Assistant Ma certo, la prendo subito. Che taglia porta?
Mary   Porto la 42.
Assistant Ecco la 42. La vuole provare?
Mary   Sì, grazie, dove sono i camerini?
Assistant Sono qui a destra.

Two minutes later she comes out and speaks to her friend Carla.

Mary   Carla, come mi sta?
Carla   Molto bene.
Mary   Sì, mi piace. La prendo.

At the shoe shop.

Client   Vorrei un paio di scarpe di pelle marrone.
Assistant Che numero porta?
Client   Porto il 38. Mi piacciono quelle lì in vetrina.
Assistant Va bene, le prendo subito.

Esercizi

1   Listen to the dialogue and complete the grid in Italian. (*Answers on page 130.*)

articolo	taglia	colore	materiale	prezzo	la compra?/non la compra?

2 Complete these sentences with the words given below. (*Answers on page 130.*)

26
36
38
Cross reference with units:

Buongiorno .... comprare un .... di scarpe .... di ....
Che .... porta?
Porto ...... 38.

Buongiorno. Vorrei comprare una ....
Sì, di che ....?
Il colore non importa ma io porto la ...... ed è .... trovare gonne per
questa ....
Un momento! Ecco. Una gonna di ....
Sì, questa .... piace.
...... vuole provare? I .... sono qui a ....

| colore | mi | vorrei | 50 | sinistra | difficile | lana | pelle |

| camerini | paio | la | nere | taglia | numero | gonna | il |

3 Role play. You are buying some shoes. Listen to the recording and complete
the dialogue following the prompts given below. The shop assistant begins by
asking what you would like. (*Answers on page 130.*)

1. Say, 'I would like a pair of shoes'.   **2.** Say 'Black'.   **3.** Say '39'.
4. Ask 'How much are they?'   **5.** Say 'I'll take them'.

Tip

da translates the English word 'for': **scarpe da uomo** 'shoes for men'. It indicates
the function or purpose, but not the content. For example **una tazza da tè** is 'a tea
cup' *but* **una tazza di tè** is 'a cup of tea'.

la prendo, lo prendo, li prendo, le prendo. To avoid repeating the name of an
object or a person, **la**, (it, her), **lo** (it, him), **li** (them, masc) or **le** (them, fem) is put
in front of the verb. Which is used depends on the number and the gender of the
object or person:

	Masc	*Fem*
Sing	il profumo: lo prendo	la gonna: la prendo
Plural	i bambini: li vedo	le scarpe: le prendo

Italians use the verb **piacere** for 'to like'. To say 'I like' they say **mi piace** (*literally*
'it is pleasing to me') or **mi piacciono** (*literally* 'they are pleasing to me'),
depending on whether what is liked is singular or plural:

La camicetta mi piace.	I like the blouse.
Le scarpe mi piacciono.	I like the shoes.

The verb **stare** with the meaning 'to suit' has a similar construction:

La camicetta mi sta bene.	The blouse suits me.
Le scarpe mi stanno bene.	The shoes suit me.

Panorama italiano

Italians are prepared to spend quite a lot of money when it comes to fashion.
They look for clothes to express their individuality but also expect them to be of
good quality. Italian advertising strongly emphasizes the relationship linking the
practical, the elegant and the exclusive!

Test yourself

Revision

1 What can be bought where? Match the item with the shop that sells it. (*Answers on page 130.*)

1 un francobollo	si compra	**A** dal giornalaio
2 un biglietto dell'autobus	si compra	**B** all'ufficio postale
3 lo sciroppo	si compra	**C** in farmacia

2 Travelling by train. Listen to the three announcements and complete the table below. (*Answers on page 130.*)

	PLATFORM	DESTINATION	OTHER INFORMATION
A			
B			
C			

3 Italian adventure. Read the story and next to each number write the letter of the missing sentence. (*Answers on page 130.*)

When Mary arrived in Rome, she went straight to the station to get a ticket to Tarquinia. On the way to the station she was stopped by a gentleman who wanted to know how to get to Piazza Esedra. '**1**......' '**2**......', replied Mary in good Italian. Then she looked at her watch and saw that it had stopped so she asked a passer-by, '**3**......?' Oh! She had to hurry if she wanted to make sure she caught the five-fifty-five train. '**4**......,' she asked the ticket officer. '**5**......?' She had ten minutes to wait so she went for a coffee. '**6**......', she said, '**7**......?' I could buy an Italian paper to read on the train, Mary thought. '**8**......' Suddenly there was an announcement, '**9**......'. She didn't quite catch the platform number. '**10**......', she asked another passenger and finally here she was, on the train to Tarquinia, ready to start her Italian adventure.

A Attenzione prego, locale per Tarquinia è in arrivo al binario sette.
B Che ore sono, per favore?
C È in orario?
D Mi dispiace, non sono di qua.
E Vorrei un giornale italiano. Questo qua: Il Messaggero.
F Un biglietto per Tarquinia
G Un caffè ed una brioche.
H Scusi, per andare a Piazza Esedra va bene sempre dritto?
I Scusi, a che binario arriva?
J Quant'è?

4 Discover the three fruit hidden in this grid. (*Answers on page 130.*)

O	B	E	F	M	F	S	A	F	E
I	A	N	G	U	R	I	A	I	L
R	A	L	B	I	C	O	C	C	A
C	M	E	R	L	O	O	M	O	G

5 Who is the suspect? Match the pictures with the descriptions below. (*Answers on page 130.*)

1   **2**   **3**

A È simpatica, alta, magra con i capelli lisci neri.
B Ha i capelli ricci biondi. È basso e grasso.
C È un ragazzo bruno, piccolo e magro. Ha i jeans neri e le scarpe sportive.

6 Colori. Listen to the three dialogues and write down in English the colours mentioned. (*Answers on page 130.*)

A .... **B** .... **C** ....
....
....

7 Puzzle. Complete the crossword. You will find the name of a tasty Italian cheese in the shaded column. (*Answers on page 130.*)

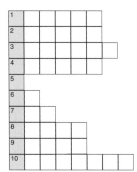

Clues **1.** ... + blu = verde **2.** Il treno è in ... (on time). **3.** Il treno è in ... (late). **4.** contrario di (opposite of) 'magro' **5.** Via aerea ... via mare? **6.** Ce ne sono due in 'sonno' e 'anno'. **7.** la sorella del papà **8.** Ha gli ... azzurri. **9.** contrario di 'corto' **10.** Bisogna pensare alle feste in ... (advance).

8 Quanto ne desidera? Ask your customer how much/many of each of the following ingredients she would like, using the correct form of **quanto**. For example 'Quante mele desidera'. (*Answers on page 130.*)

A **B** **C** **D** **E** **F**

9 Insert **Mi piace** or **Mi piacciono** to complete the sentences below. *(Answers on page 130.)*

1 ... il rosso. **2** ... quelle scarpe nere. **3** ... questa vetrina.
4 ... i profumi intensi. **5** ... i ragazzi alti. **6** ... quella gonna verde.

10 Look at the pictures and read the descriptions. Then write in the name of each person and the description for Anna and Leonardo. (*Answers on page 130.*)

A **B** **C** **D** **E** **F** **G** **H** **I**

Gabrio è biondo. Porta i jeans e la maglia nera.
Emanuela è bruna e magra. La sua gonna è corta.
Gianna è bionda. Ha una gonna nera e corta.
Antonietta è grassa. La sua gonna è lunga.
Paolo porta la maglia e i pantaloni.
Michele è un bambino bruno, porta i pantaloni corti.
Marco è bruno. La sua camicia è bianca.

Shopping

At the supermarket

Vocabolario

di cosa abbiamo bisogno?	what do we need?
abbiamo bisogno di ...	we need ...
le olive	olives
il pannolino	nappy
quale? quali?	which?
dolce	mild
saporito, saporita	savoury
in offerta	on special offer
assaggiare	to taste
pecorino, ricotta	types of cheese
voglio (volere)	I want
la confezione	pack
la salumeria	delicatessen
i funghi	mushrooms
secco, secca, secchi, secche	dried

Dialoghi

Letizia and Donatella go to the supermarket.

Letizia	Di cosa abbiamo bisogno?
Donatella	Abbiamo bisogno di caffè, zucchero, olive e formaggio. Il formaggio che vendono qui è molto buono.
Letizia	Io ho bisogno di pannolini per Giacomo.
Donatella	Ecco i pannolini. Quali vuoi?
Letizia	Quelli là.

At the cheese counter.

Assistant	Prego?
Donatella	Un etto di olive.
Assistant	Quali? Vuole queste verdi o quelle nere?
Donatella	Quelle nere, per favore.
Assistant	Altro?
Letizia	Sì, del formaggio. Tre etti di pecorino.
Assistant	Vuole il pecorino dolce o quello saporito?
Letizia	Preferisco quello saporito.
Assistant	Volete assaggiare questa ricotta? È molto saporita ed è in offerta.

Esercizi

1 Complete the sentences with the correct form of **quello**. (*Answers on page 130.*)

il caffè	Vuole questo? No, voglio ....
il formaggio	Vuole questo? No, voglio ....
lo zucchero	Vuole questo? No, voglio ....
i pannolini	Vuole questi? No, voglio ....
le olive	Vuole queste? No, voglio ....
la ricotta	Vuole questa? No, voglio ....

2 Keen pricing. Listen to announcements giving the prices of special offers and complete the table. *(Answers on page 130.)*

	PREZZO
acqua minerale: la bottiglia	....
olive: all'etto	....
tè alla pesca: 3 bottiglie	....
spaghetti: ½ kg	....
caffè: 250 g	....
funghi secchi: una confezione	....
1 salame	....

3 Role play. Imagine you are Mrs Mazzini and use the shopping list below to ask for goods at your local **salumeria** (delicatessen). Ask for one item at a time in the order of the list. The shopkeeper starts by saying good morning and asking what you would like. *(Answers on page 130.)*

> 1 pack yoghurt
> 2 packs tortellini
> 1 packet butter
> 1 pack dried mushrooms
> 200 g pecorino cheese
> 1 bottle white wine
> 1 packet pasta

Tip

quale (m/f sing) and **quali** (m/f plur) are used in questions. They mean 'which?'. They can be adjectives (i.e. followed by a noun) or pronouns (i.e. used on their own). **Quale** shortens to **Qual** in the expression **Qual è ...?** 'Which is ...?'

Quale formaggio vuoi?	**Quale vuoi?**
A quale salumeria vai?	**A quale vai?**
Quali pannolini compri?	**Quali compri?**
Quali olive preferisci?	**Quali preferisci?**

Panorama italiano

A **salumeria** sells all sorts of cold pork meats (**salumi**), cheeses, tinned and bottled products, and often a variety of ready made dishes from starters to main courses.

Away from home

Booking a room and enquiring about hotel facilities

Vocabolario

la camera	room	gennaio	January
il bagno	bathroom	febbraio	February
la doccia	shower	marzo	March
il parcheggio	car park	aprile	April
il giardino	garden	maggio	May
la televisione	television	giugno	June
il frigobar	fridge	luglio	July
doppia	twin bedroom	agosto	August
singola	single bedroom	settembre	September
matrimoniale	double bedroom	ottobre	October
		novembre	November
la mezza pensione	half board	dicembre	December
la pensione completa	full board		
la colazione	breakfast		
il pernottamento	overnight accommodation		
confermare	to confirm		
conferma	confirmation		
la data	date		
la prenotazione	booking, reservation		
sapere	to know		
inoltre	as well		

Dialogo

Mr Corbetta rings Hotel Primavera to book rooms for a holiday in Maratea.

Receptionist	Buongiorno, Hotel Primavera.
Signor Corbetta	Buongiorno, vorrei prenotare una camera doppia e due camere singole per luglio.
Receptionist	Per quali date in luglio?
Signor Corbetta	Dunque, dal primo al 15 di luglio.
Receptionist	Desidera prenotare mezza pensione, pensione completa o solo pernottamento?
Signor Corbetta	Vorrei la mezza pensione, se possibile. Quanto costano le camere con la mezza pensione?
Receptionist	Allora, la doppia viene 83.500 e la singola 60.000.
Signor Corbetta	Avete un parcheggio?
Receptionist	Sì, abbiamo un parcheggio ed anche un giardino per i bambini.
Signor Corbetta	Benissimo. Allora vorrei confermare la prenotazione.
Receptionist	Va bene, signore. Il suo nome prego?

Esercizi

1 Listen to the description of the hotel and tick the facilities and other benefits available. (*Answers on page 130.*)

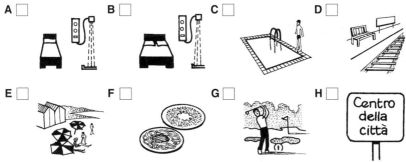

A ☐   B ☐   C ☐   D ☐

E ☐   F ☐   G ☐   H ☐

2 Complete this letter of confirmation for a booking in Taormina using the list of words on the right. (*Answers on page 130.*)

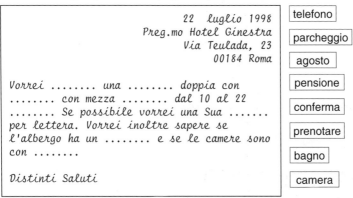

22   luglio 1998
Preg.mo Hotel Ginestra
Via Teulada, 23
00184 Roma

Vorrei .... una .... doppia con
.... con mezza .... dal 10 al 22
.... Se possibile vorrei una Sua ....
per lettera. Vorrei inoltre sapere se
l'albergo ha un .... e se le camere sono
con ....

Distinti Saluti

telefono

parcheggio

agosto

pensione

conferma

prenotare

bagno

camera

3 Ring Hotel Miramare and make a booking. Follow the prompts given below. The receptionist starts by saying good morning. (*Answers on page 130.*)

1. Say, 'Hello I would like to book a double room'.   **2.** Say 'From 23 till 30 of May'.   **3.** Ask 'How much is it with breakfast?'   **4.** Say 'OK. Is it far from the beach?'   **5.** Say 'I would like to book'.

Tip

Names of months are written in lower case.
When you say the date you use: **il due agosto** August 2nd, **l'otto maggio** May 8th. Where English uses ordinal numbers (first, second, etc.) Italian uses cardinal numbers: **il nove settembre** (*literally* the nine September); the exception is the first of the month, where you use **il primo**: **il primo aprile** the first of April.

Panorama italiano

Hotels
When you book a hotel room you need to send a deposit of the equivalent of 2 to 3 days of your stay. If you need to book accommodation in advance in Italy try the **Azienda di Soggiorno/Azienda Autonoma del Turismo/Azienda di Promozione Turistica** or **APT** (Tourist Board), **Ufficio Informazioni** (Information Office) and **Pro Loco** (local tourist office).

UNIT 45

Away from home

Camping and campsite facilities

Vocabolario

il campeggio	campsite, camping
ce n'è uno	there is one of them
appena	just
fuori	outside
il paese	village
le indicazioni	signs
il posto	place, space
la tenda	tent
un posto tenda	a space for a tent
una canadese	a tent for two
la patente	driving licence
le attrezzature	facilities
accesso	access
la piantina	map
il campo da tennis (i campi …)	tennis court (tennis courts)
la sala da giochi	games room
il cancello	gate
rientrare	to go/come back in
la piscina	swimming pool
tranquillo	quiet

Dialoghi

Linda and Paul are looking for a campsite.

Linda C'è un campeggio qui vicino?

Passer-by Sì, ce n'è uno appena fuori dal paese. Lei deve seguire le indicazioni per Padova e lo trova sulla sinistra. È il campeggio 'Tre Laghi'.

Linda Grazie.

At the campsite.

Paul Buongiorno, avete un posto tenda libero?

Receptionist Sì, per che tenda?

Paul È una canadese per due persone.

Receptionist Bene. Ho bisogno di un documento: carta d'identità, passaporto, patente …

Paul Ecco i nostri passaporti.

Linda enquires about the camping facilities.

Linda Che attrezzature ha il campeggio?

Manager Il campeggio ha un campo da tennis, una sala giochi, un bar, un ristorante ed un minimarket. Le docce sono con acqua calda e fredda e sono vicino al campo da tennis. Ecco una piantina del campeggio.

Linda E quanto costa?

Manager Allora il prezzo è di diecimila lire al giorno e questo comprende libero accesso a tutte le attrezzature del campeggio.

Linda Grazie. E il campeggio chiude la sera?

Manager Sì, chiudiamo l'entrata principale a mezzanotte ma voi avete la chiave per rientrare. Ecco la chiave del cancello.

Esercizi

1 Listen to the conversation. Tick the facilities that are available and put a cross next to those that are not. (*Answers on page 130.*)

1. mare ☐ **5.** posti tenda ☐ **9.** supermercato ☐
2. campi da tennis ☐ **6.** posti camper ☐ **10.** piscina ☐
3. bar ☐ **7.** posti roulotte ☐ **11.** giardino per bambini ☐
4. ristorante ☐ **8.** acqua fredda/calda ☐

2 Complete the crossword. In the shaded column you will find the name of an item useful for when you go camping. (*Answers on page 130.*)

Clues 1. a tent for two (+ definite article) **2.** entrance, access **3.** unscramble this word: ADENT **4.** Che .... sono? Le due e mezza. **5.** to come back in **6.** Il .... principale chiude a mezzanotte. **7.** one of the sports facilities (plural + definite article) **8.** It could be hot or cold.

3 You are looking for a space at a campsite. Follow the prompts provided below. The manager starts by saying good morning. (*Answers on page 130.*)

1. Ask 'Is there a free space for a tent for two?' **2.** Say 'For a week'. **3.** Say 'Here is my passport'; then ask 'What facilities does the campsite have?' **4.** Ask 'Is it quiet in the evening?'

Tip

tutto is followed by the article **il, la**, etc:

tutto il giorno all day **tutte le mattine** every morning **tutta l'acqua** all the water

la sera means 'in the evening'. It can be used instead of **di sera**. The same applies to **mattina, pomeriggio, notte**:

La mattina prendo un caffè. In the morning I drink coffee.

The combination of **c'è** (there is) and **ne** ('of it/them') results in **ce n'è**; **ce n'è uno** means 'there is one of them'. The combination of **ci sono** ('there are') and **ne** results in **ce ne sono**; **ce ne sono due** means 'there are two of them'.

Panorama italiano

Italians and holidays
Italians like travelling and tend to book their holidays well in advance. Avoid Italy in August if you suffer in the heat and remember that on 15th August (a holiday called **Ferragosto**) everything is closed for at least three days.

People

Talking about your daily routine

Vocabolario

mi sveglio (svegliarsi)	I wake up
mi alzo (alzarsi)	I get up
mi lavo (lavarsi)	I get washed
mi vesto (vestirsi)	I get dressed
faccio colazione (fare)	I have breakfast
ascolto (ascoltare)	I listen to
uscire	to go out
pranzo (pranzare)	I have lunch
cenare	to have dinner
fare la spesa	to do the shopping
guardo la televisione (guardare)	I watch TV
riprendo (riprendere)	I start again
la vita	life
tranquillo, tranquilla	quiet
movimentato, movimentata	busy
che	that
adesso	now
di solito	usually
qualche volta	sometimes
poi	then
mi	myself
ti	yourself (*informal*)
si	himself, herself, itself
	oneself, yourself (*formal*)
ci	ourselves
vi	yourselves
si	themselves (*formal and informal*)

Dialoghi

Federica asks her friend Luca what his day is like, now that he is working.

Federica Com'è la tua giornata?

Luca È una giornata abbastanza movimentata. Mi sveglio alle sette, mi alzo alle sette e un quarto, mi lavo, mi vesto e faccio colazione con un caffè. Alle otto arrivo in ufficio, lavoro fino alle 12.30, poi pranzo al bar. Riprendo il lavoro all'una e mezza e finisco alle 17.00. E la tua giornata com'è, Federica?

It is now Federica's turn to tell us about her day.

Federica La mia giornata è tranquilla. Lavoro solo di mattina dalle nove all'una. Rientro, preparo il pranzo, guardo il telegiornale o ascolto la radio. Qualche volta vado a fare la spesa. La sera guardo la televisione e qualche volta vado al cinema.

Luca E a che ora ti alzi la mattina?

Federica Abito vicino all'ufficio, 10 minuti a piedi. Di solito mi alzo alle 8.00.

Esercizi

1   Listen to Marcella's routine and put the pictures below in the correct order.
(*Answers on page 130.*)

A   **B**   **C**   **D**

2   Unscramble the following sentences. (*Answers on page 130.*)

1. a riprendo tre lavorare alle
2. di la solito televisione guardo
3. spesa qualche vado a fare la volta
4. vesto mi
5. quando telegiornale guardo il ceno

3   Role play. Imagine you are Lorenzo. Listen to the recording and answer the
questions about your day using the prompts below. The interviewer starts by
asking you at what time you usually get up. (*Answers on page 130.*)

1. Get up at 7.00.   **2.** Leave the house at 7.40.   **3.** Go to work by car.
4. Start work at 8.00.   **5.** Have lunch in the office.   **6.** Watch TV.

Tip

The reflexive pronouns are **mi** ('myself'), **ti** ('yourself' informal), **si** ('himself',
'herself', 'itself', 'yourself' formal), **ci** ('ourselves'), **vi** ('yourselves' formal and
informal"), **si** ('themselves'). Verbs that can be used in the reflexive are shown in
the dictionary with **-si** on the end, e.g. **alzarsi** ('to get up'). The **-si** means 'oneself'!
For 'I', 'you', etc., put the correct pronoun before the correct form of the verb:

mi alzo	**ci alziamo**
ti alzi	**vi alzate**
si alza	**si alzano**

Panorama italiano

Italians tend to have a very quick breakfast which consists of a **cappuccino** or an
espresso or **caffellatte** ('milk and coffee') with some biscuits or a **cornetto**
('croissant'). Most of the time breakfast is consumed in a cafe before going to
work. Lunch is around 1.00–1.30 and the evening meal at 8.00–8.30.

 **Leisure**

Hobbies and leisure activities

Vocabolario

leggere	to read
scrivere	to write
ballare	to dance
cantare	to sing
ascoltare	to listen to
fare collezione di } **fare raccolta di**	to collect
fare sport	to practise sport
incontrare amici	to meet friends
giocare	to play (*sport, game*)
suonare	to play (*instrument*)
francobolli	stamps
libri antichi	old books
la musica	music
la radio	radio
la chitarra	guitar
il sax	saxophone
classico, classica	classical
moderno, moderna	modern
il complesso	group

 ### Dialogo

Marta and Marco exchange information about their interests.

Marta Che cosa fai nel tempo libero?
Marco Mi piace leggere, scrivere, ascoltare la musica.
Marta Che musica preferisci?
Marco La musica moderna. Mi piace molto la musica inglese. E tu, Marta, ascolti la musica?
Marta Sì, mi piace, però preferisco ballare e fare sport e camminare e quando ho soldi, vado al cinema e a teatro.

Giorgio has written a letter to Pietro about his interests.

> Nel tempo libero mi piace incontrare gli amici e andare a ballare. Ho un computer e mi piace giocare con i videogames. Faccio anche raccolta di francobolli internazionali. Mi piace ascoltare la radio. Suono il sax e la chitarra e mi piace viaggiare.

Esercizi

1   Listen to Nicoletta and Daniele talking about their hobbies and then write
    their names under the pictures below. (*Answers on page 130.*)

A _____   **B** _____

2   Match the Italian words with the English equivalents. (*Answers on page 130.*)

A leggere   **1** walking
B scrivere   **2** collecting stamps
C camminare   **3** reading
D fare collezione di francobolli **4** doing sport
E fare sport   **5** writing

3   Listen to the recording and answer Margherita's questions about your hobbies
    using the prompts below. She speaks first. (*Answers on page 130.*)

1. Say 'I like to do sport, I like walking and travelling'.   **2.** Say 'Yes, and
I prefer classical music'.   **3.** Say 'Yes, I like to go the cinema and the theatre'.

Tip

Although **radio** ends in **-o** it is feminine (*la* **radio**), while **cinema** ends in **-a** but is
masculine (*il* **cinema**). The word 'cinema' comes from Greek. Most 'borrowed'
words take the masculine articles **il, lo, l'** (singular), **i, gli** (plural):

**il bar   il computer   il disk jockey   il rugby   lo swatch   l'e-mail
i videogames   gli Euro   But   la hit-parade   la hi-fi   la jeep**

The question word **che** is invariable:

Che musica preferisci?   Che libri preferisci?

Panorama italiano

Italian television
Italians watch a lot television either as a family activity or in public areas (trattorie,
bars, the square, etc.) in the case of national events. There is a wide variety of
television channels and programmes.

UNIT 48 Leisure

More about sports and hobbies

Vocabolario

lo sci	skiing
la pallavolo	volleyball
la pallacanestro	basketball
il nuoto	swimming
il calcio	football
il ciclismo	cycling
il footing	jogging
il ping pong	table tennis
la vela	sailing
il villaggio	the tourist club
giocare a ...	to play ... (a sport)
sciare	to ski
nuotare	to swim
cavalcare	to ride
la squadra	team
la partita	match
il torneo	competition
fare il tifo per ...	to be a supporter of ... (football team)
allo stadio	at the stadium

Dialoghi

Lidia and Gabrio talk about football.

Lidia	Gabrio, per quale squadra fai il tifo?
Gabrio	Io faccio il tifo per la Juventus e tu?
Lidia	Io per l'Inter. Guardi la partita stasera?
Gabrio	Sì, e vado anche allo stadio oggi pomeriggio.

Manuela and Cristiano talk about their hobbies.

Manuela	Cristiano, qui al villaggio si possono fare molti sport. Andiamo a fare vela oggi?
Cristiano	Sì, va bene. Vorrei anche fare un po' di footing. Vieni con me?
Manuela	Sì, va bene. A che ora?
Cristiano	Alle 7.00. Facciamo footing in spiaggia, OK?
Manuela	Buona idea! Questa sera c'è una partita di pallavolo. Andiamo?
Cristiano	Non posso, perché c'è il torneo di ping pong.

Enrico and Gabriella talk about their hobbies.

Enrico	Mi piace sciare, nuotare e cavalcare quando fa bel tempo. E tu che cosa fai?
Gabriella	Mi piace nuotare, gioco a pallavolo e mi piace fare vela quando sono in vacanza.

Esercizi

1 Listen to Paola and Marco talking about the sports they do. Complete the grid by ticking which sports they mention and when they like to do them. (*Answers on page 131.*)

	PAOLA		MARCO	
pallacanestro				
pallavolo				
nuoto				
sci				
footing				
ping pong				
cavalcare				
vela				

2 Match the couples. Massimo, Alberto and Giorgio's wives are Valeria, Margherita and Carla, but not necessarily in this order. Margherita and Valeria are sisters. Use the information below to work out who is married to whom. (*Answers on page 131.*)

Il marito di Carla è l'unico che non fa sport.
Massimo gioca a tennis ma non gli piace il calcio.
Alberto, il marito di Valeria, gioca a calcio e va a sciare. Gioca molto bene a tennis.
Valeria e Margherita giocano spesso a tennis con i mariti.

Husbands	Wives
Massimo Alberto Giorgio	

3 Write in Italian what Massimo and Giovanna like doing according to the profiles below. (*Answers on page 131.*)

Massimo   likes swimming, riding and skiing
Giovanna   is a supporter of Sampdoria, likes sailing and playing volleyball.

Tip

You will remember that in Italian there are three types of verbs: **-are, -ere** and **-ire** and they follow a regular pattern. But within each of these there are irregular verbs:

fare ('to make', 'to do'):	**faccio** I make, I do
potere ('to be able to'):	**possono** they can
venire ('to come'):	**vieni** you come
andare ('to go'):	**va** he/she/it goes

Panorama italiano

Gli italiani e lo sport

In recent years there has been an increase in the popularity of and participation in sports like tennis, volleyball, athletics and skiing. In the north more than half the population ski and play basketball, while in the south football is the most popular sport. Many sports have very ancient roots and in many regions they are relived at different times of the year in period costume. One example is **il Palio** in Siena, which is a horse race.

Test yourself

Revision

1 Michela is having a dinner party. Listen to the recording and write down in Italian the ingredients she needs to buy. (*Answers on page 131.*)

2 Room with a view. Look at these hotel brochures. You have two children and would like to avoid having to cross roads to get to the beach. A family-run hotel with a garden for the children and not too noisy would be ideal. Select the most suitable hotel and explain in English why the others are not suitable. (*Answers on page 131.*)

VILLA CARLOTTA

Ideale per il riposo.

—

Zona tranquilla nei boschi.

—

500 m. dalla spiaggia.

—

Hotel Miramare

Hotel di 1ª categoria.
Ristorante.

La spiaggia è a 200 m. dall'altra parte della Via Aurelia.

Pensione Gardena

Pensione familiare.
•
Grande giardino.
•
Di fronte alla spiaggia.
•
Zona tranquilla.

A ....
B ....
C ....

3 Textsalad. Rearrange these six sentences in the correct order to form the dialogue. (*Answers on page 131.*)

1 Mezza pensione o pensione completa?
2 Dal diciotto agosto al tre settembre.
3 Desidera?
4 Vorrei prenotare una camera doppia.
5 Pensione completa.
6 Per quando?

4 Camping. You are not happy with the campsite. Look at the pictures below and complain to the manager about the facilities that are missing or unsatisfactory. (*Answers on page 131.*)

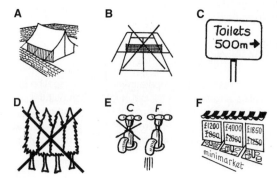

A B C Toilets 500m →

D E F minimarket

5 Listen to the tape and write in English a description of Mariella's day. (*Answers on page 131.*)

6 Based on Esercizio 5, write a brief letter in Italian describing your own day. (*Sample answer on page 131.*)

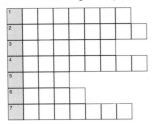

Cara Maria,

7 Stretch yourself! Insert the correct form of the verb in the sentences below. (*Answers on page 131.*)

  1 Roberto, che cosa ... nel tempo libero?   (fare)
  2 Mamma, a che ora ... a lavorare Marco?   (cominciare)
  3 Che musica ..., Giovanna?   (ascoltare)
  4 (Io) ... molto sport.   (fare)
  5 Serena, Carla, ... spesso al cinema?   (andare)
  6 (Noi) ... ogni sabato.   (andare)
  7 Carlo, (noi) ... bisogno di caffè.   (avere)
  8 ... (voi) assaggiare questo pecorino dolce?   (volere)
  9 Io ... sempre presto.   (alzarsi)
10 A che ora ... tu?   (cenare)

8 Sports and hobbies. Complete the crossword. In the shaded column you will find the name of a game. *(Answers on page 131.)*

Clues 1 Mi piace molto ... (to write). **2** Mi piace ... (to walk). **3** ... (listen to) musica classica, Carlo? **4** Faccio sempre ... alle sette e mezza. **5** La sera ... alle otto. **6** Questo ... (hotel) non mi piace. **7** Quando ...... (meet) i tuoi amici?

Away from home

Different holidays and facilities

Vocabolario

la roulotte	caravan
il camper	camper
il bungalow	bungalow
la lezione	lesson
il sacco a pelo	sleeping bag
la lavanderia a gettoni	launderette
l'istruttore	instructor
il paesaggio	scenery, landscape
la zanzara	mosquito
pulito	clean
all'estero	abroad
decidere	to decide
vorresti ...?	would you like ...?
che ne dici di ...?	what about ...?
che ne dici di andare in Scozia?	what about going to Scotland?

Dialoghi

Marco and Sabrina are discussing what they are going to do during their summer holiday.

Marco   Sabrina, dobbiamo decidere cosa fare quest'estate. Tu, dove vorresti andare?

Sabrina   Veramente, non lo so. Vorrei provare ad andare all'estero quest'anno. Che ne dici di andare in Scozia?

Marco   Buona idea. Ma andiamo con la roulotte!

Sabrina   Certo, così possiamo vedere il paesaggio!

The Rossinis are deciding about their holiday.

Signora Rossini   Valerio, allora dove prenotiamo quest'anno? Ancora a Riva degli Etruschi?

Signor Rossini   Ma sì. I bambini conoscono tutti, ci sono molte attività ricreative, sport per gli adulti, l'istruttore di windsurf, nuoto, tennis. C'è il bar sul mare, il supermercato, i negozi, la nursery, la lavanderia a gettoni. I bambini si divertono, il mare è buono.

Signora Rossini   Sì, hai ragione, poi c'è la pineta che rinfresca e non ci sono zanzare! Allora prenoto ancora il bungalow 310 vicino al mare.

Esercizi

1   Listen to two people talking about their holiday plans and complete the grid below in English. (*Answers on page 131.*)

	Signora Angelini	Riccardo
1 When		
2 Facilities		
3 Other features		

2 Complete the crossword and in the shaded column you will find a useful new word to do with holidays. (*Answers on page 131.*)

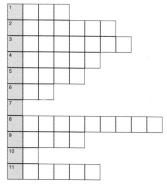

Clues   **1** dalle tre … quattro   **2** Mi piace … a tennis.   **3** Non vado in camper ma in ….   **4** Roma è in ….   **5** una canadese   **6** È l'… (1.00).   **7** Ce ne sono due in **vorresti**.   **8** C'è anche l' … di nuoto.   **9** Dormi nel … a pelo?   **10** … piace il mare (I like).   **11** non in ritardo, in …

3 Now it is your turn to discuss your holidays with Alessandra. Follow the prompts below. She starts by asking you what kind of holidays you prefer. (*Answers on page 131.*)

1. Say 'I like the seaside best'.   **2.** Say 'This year I would like to go abroad'.   **3.** Say 'In July or September'.

Tip

conoscere and **sapere** both mean 'to know'. **conoscere** is used for places or people:

> **Conosco Marco**. I know Mark.   **Conosco Firenze**. I know Florence.

sapere is used for 'knowing a fact' or 'knowing how to do something':

> **So parlare francese**.   I know (how to speak) French.
> **So come andare a Roma**.   I know how to get to Rome.

Grammar practice
Fill in the gaps with the correct form of **conoscere** or **sapere**. (*Answers on page 131.*)

1 **Non … se Marco … Edinburgo.** I don't know if Mark knows Edinburgh.
2 **Io … come arrivare a Lucca ma non … l'indirizzo esatto di Giovanni.** I know how to get to Lucca but I don't know Giovanni's exact address.
3 **Marco … giocare a tennis ma non … bene le regole del gioco.** Marco knows how to play tennis but does not know the rules well.

Panorama italiano

Italian school holidays
In most regions, schools close from the middle of June to the middle of September. Italian families tend to go on holiday some time during that period. Children also have two weeks holiday at Christmas and two at Easter. There is no half term.

Leisure

Visiting friends, describing accommodation

Vocabolario

la casa	house, home
l'appartamento	flat
la terrazza	terrace, balcony
l'anticamera	entrance hall
la sala	lounge
la camera da letto	bedroom
il corridoio	hall
la cucina	kitchen
la scala	stairs
la mansarda	converted attic
lo studio	study
che bel/bello/bella	what a beautiful
da quanto tempo	how long
(venite) avanti	come in
passate (passare)	you spend, do you spend?
muoio dalla voglia di ...	I'm dying to ...
state (stare)	do you live, have you been living?
non restate (restare)	don't remain
su	upstairs
di prima	former
mq	m^2

Dialogo

Gianni and Marina are going to visit Simona and Maurizio's new flat.

Marina	Simona, Maurizio, che bell'appartamento! Da quanto tempo state qua?
Simona	Grazie, stiamo qua da un anno.
Maurizio	Venite avanti, non restate in anticamera. Ecco, questa è la sala.
Marina	Che bella terrazza, così grande!
Simona	Sì, passiamo molto tempo in terrazza, mangiamo in terrazza e Matteo gioca in terrazza.
Marina	Simona, muoio dalla voglia di vedere tutta la casa.
Simona	Certo, vieni con me. Dietro la sala c'è la cucina. Poi questa qui a destra è la camera di Matteo e quella di fronte a sinistra è la nostra camera da letto. In fondo al corridoio ci sono due bagni, uno più grande e uno più piccolo. E lì è la scala per la mansarda; vieni su con me.
Marina	Che bello studio con terrazza!
Simona	Sì, lo studio è anche camera per gli ospiti e c'è un piccolo bagno con doccia.
Marina	Che bella casa, Simona, più bella di quella di prima. Sono contenta per voi.

Esercizi

1 Comparing sizes. Read the information opposite and decide who has the largest and who has the smallest room. (see **Tip** if you need help.) (*Answers on page 131.*)

La camera di Gabrio è meno grande della camera di Vieri. La camera di Paolo è più grande della camera di Gabrio. La camera di Vieri è più grande della camera di Paolo.

2   Listen to the dialogue again and label the rooms on the plan with the appropriate letter. (*Answers on page 131.*)

A l'anticamera
B la sala
C la camera di Matteo
D la camera da letto di Simona e Maurizio
E il corridoio
F il bagno
G la cucina
H la scala per la mansarda

3   La mia casa. Prepare a short oral presentation in Italian about the place where you live. Say how long you have been living there, the number of rooms, their relative locations and their relative sizes.

4   Stretch yourself. Write a short passage comparing your house with the house of your dreams.

Tip

When **bello** (beautiful) precedes the noun it describes it has forms similar to those of **il** and **quel**:

bell'appartamento   bello studio   bel bagno   bella terrazza

più ('more') and **meno** ('less') are used to compare people and things. **di** or **che** are used to say 'than'. Generally you use **di** before nouns, pronouns and numbers and **che** in all other cases.

Questa stanza è più grande di quella.	This room is larger than that one.
Questa stanza è meno larga che lunga.	This room is less wide than long.

Panorama italiano

Italians prefer to live in the town centre. Flats and penthouses are the most expensive and sought-after types of accommodation. Property advertisements give details of the rooms and their sizes in square metres:

Appartamento mq 150 con mansarda e terrazza ...
Flat of 150 m² with converted attic and terrace ...

Information

Enquiring about recipes

Vocabolario

le penne	type of pasta
la ricetta	recipe
lo zafferano	saffron
il basilico	basil
la passata	sieved tomatoes
pronto, pronta	ready, ready-made
il sale	salt
sciogliere	to melt
il brodo	stock
bollire	to boil
la pentola	pot, pan
rosolare	to brown
l'aglio	garlic
aggiungere	to add
cuocere	to cook
scolare	to drain
versare	to pour
mescolare	to stir
fumante	steaming
il peperoncino	chilli pepper

Dialogo

Mrs Rossi talks to Mr Gestori about her new recipe 'Penne alla Mario'.

Signora Rossi   Signor Gestori, ho una nuova ricetta per Lei.

Signor Gestori   Sentiamo! Che cosa occorre?

Signora Rossi   È una ricetta molto semplice e veloce da fare. Allora, si prende un chilo di pasta, precisamente un chilo di penne, dello zafferano, un po' di basilico, della passata pronta, sale e parmigiano.

Signor Gestori   E quando si mette lo zafferano?

Signora Rossi   Allora, si fa sciogliere lo zafferano in un po' di brodo e intanto si fa bollire una pentola con molta acqua. Quando l'acqua bolle si aggiunge del sale e si cuoce la pasta. Intanto si fa rosolare l'aglio in un po' d'olio e si aggiunge della passata. Quando la pasta è pronta si scola e si versa nella pentola della salsa, si aggiunge lo zafferano, si mette un po' di basilico, si mescola e si serve fumante con del parmigiano.

Esercizi

 1   Listen to the recipe on the radio and arrange the stages in the correct order. (*Answers on page 131.*)

A   **B**   **C**   **D**

2 Insert the correct word, based on the recipe in Esercizio 1. (*Answers on page 131.*)

...... bollire l'acqua in una pentola; quando l'acqua ......, si aggiunge ...... sale. Poi ...... l'aglio e si fa ...... in un po' ...... olio. Questa salsa ...... sugli spaghetti.

3 Listen to the recording and answer the questions about the Italian recipe using the prompts below. Your friend speaks first. (*Answers on page 131.*)

1. Say 'It takes about 15 minutes'.   **2.** Say 'One needs a kilo of spaghetti, some garlic, some oil and some chilli pepper'.

Tip

Remember that **un po' di** corresponds to 'some' in English:

un po' di sale	some salt
un po' di patatine	some crisps

You can also use **del, dello, dell', della, dei, degli, delle** to say 'some':

dello zafferano	some saffron
della salsa	some sauce

si is the equivalent of the English 'one' (or 'we', 'they', 'people'). It is followed by the third person singular of the verb.

Qui si mangia bene.	One eats well here.

You can use a similar construction, but including a noun as well. If the noun is singular then the third person singular of the verb is used; if the noun is plural the third person plural is used:

Si cuoce la pasta.	One cooks the pasta.
Si aggiungono gli spaghetti.	You add the spaghetti.

Panorama italiano

La cucina italiana
Italian cuisine is very simple, varied and suitable for vegetarians as well as meat eaters. There are many regional variations in the range of vegetables and spices as well as in the combination of dishes. The 'Mediterranean diet' is considered by the medical profession to be very healthy.
You will see that there are very specialised shops from the **Casa del formaggio** (specialising in cheeses) to the **Salumeria** (specialising in hams, salami, etc.)

Travel

Enquiring about hiring a car

Dialoghi

Mr and Mrs Beech have just landed at Pisa airport and want to hire a car.

Mrs Beech	Buongiorno, vorremmo noleggiare una macchina per una settimana. Che cosa è disponibile?
Avis representative	Vediamo un po'! Abbiamo una Mercedes 180, una Lancia Tema ...
Mrs Beech	Avete una macchina di cilindrata più piccola? Una Golf, una Fiat Punto?
Avis representative	Sì, abbiamo una Punto. È nuova, comoda ed ha un ampio bagagliaio.
Mrs Beech	Scusi, qui si accettano carte di credito?

Mrs Beech stops at a petrol station and asks how to get to Lucca.

Mrs Beech	Scusi, come si fa per andare da qui a Lucca?
Attendant	Allora, gira a destra e segue le indicazioni per l'autostrada. Sono le indicazioni in verde. Se si seguono le indicazioni per l'autostrada non si può sbagliare e poi c'è proprio l'uscita per Lucca Centro. Si deve prendere il biglietto al casello di entrata e si paga all'uscita.
Mrs Beech	Grazie, può controllare l'olio e le gomme per favore?

Five minutes later.

Attendant	La macchina ha l'olio e le gomme a posto ed il serbatoio è pieno. Buon viaggio!

Esercizi

1   Listen to the announcements and match them with the appropriate pictures. (*Answers on page 131.*)

A   B   C   D

2   Insert the correct form in the singular or plural. (*Answers on page 131.*)

   1   Si .... solo contanti. (accettare)
   2   Si .... le gomme. (controllare)
   3   Si .... automobili. (noleggiare)
   4   Si .... solo prodotti naturali. (usare)
   5   Si .... un ottimo servizio. (offrire)

3   Ask for the following information in Italian. (*Answers on page 131.*)

   1   I'd like to hire a car. I'd like an Italian car.
   2   How do I get to the motorway to Milan?
   3   40 litres of unleaded petrol, please.
   4   Can you check the tyres and the oil, please?

Tip

When a sentence contains **si** (meaning 'one', 'people') and a noun in the plural, the third person plural of the verb is used:

Si accettano carte di credito.	We accept credit cards.
Se si seguono le indicazioni …	If one follows the signs …

come si fa ('how can one)' is followed by **per** or **a** and the infinitive:

Come si fa per andare lì?	How can one go there?
Come si fa a imparare l'italiano?	How can one learn Italian?

Panorama italiano

Le strade e le autostrade italiane

In Italy motorway signs are green and 'A' road signs are blue – the other way round to UK signs! Petrol stations usually have an attendant who serves you and asks if you want the oil and the tyres checked. For petrol, you can ask for **cinquantamila** (50.000 lire), or for the amount of petrol in litres or for **il pieno** ('fill it up'). Where there is a self-service sign the attendant will not be present and petrol might be cheaper. Watch out for the sign 'Self-service' when you enter the service area.

Information

Speaking on the phone

Vocabolario

pronto?	hello?
chiamare	to call
riprovare	to try again
cosa fai domani?	what are you doing tomorrow?
telefono (telefonare)	I'll ring
stasera	tonight
passare	to put through, to put on
malissimo	very badly
ti sento malissimo	I hear you very badly (I can't hear you very well)
disturbato	bad (*telephone connection*)
forte	loud
la cabina telefonica	telephone box
la moneta (le monete)	change, coins
richiamare	to call back
chi parla?	who's speaking?
non importa	it doesn't matter
glielo	him/it to him; him/it to her
me lo	him/it to me
te lo	him/it to you
un passaggio	lift (*by car*)
dopo	later

Dialoghi

Here are a few people talking on the phone.

Giulio	Pronto?, Sono Giulio, c'è Francesco?
Francesco's mother	Ciao, Giulio, mi dispiace ma Francesco è fuori. Rientra dopo le otto. Ti deve chiamare quando rientra?
Giulio	No, non importa, riprovo io. Grazie, signora, arrivederLa.

Marta	Pronto, chi parla?
Giusi	Ciao, Marta, sono Giusi, come stai?
Marta	Ciao, Giusi. Cosa fai domani? Vai alla festa?
Giusi	Penso di sì, e tu?
Marta	Sì. Viene anche Alessandro?
Giusi	Non lo so, gli telefono stasera. Ciao a domani.

Piero	Sì?
Giusi	Ciao, Ale, sono Giusi.
Piero	No, non sono Ale, sono Piero. Te lo passo subito.

Massimo	Pronto, Carla! Mi senti?
Carla	Ti sento malissimo. La linea è disturbata. Parla più forte.
Massimo	Sono in una cabina telefonica e ho poche monete. Ti richiamo da casa.

Esercizi

1 Listen to three telephone calls and match them with the pictures. *(Answers on page 131.)*

A _____   **B** _____   **C** _____

2 Complete the crossword and in the shaded column you will find another useful word linked with telephones! *(Answers on page 131.)*

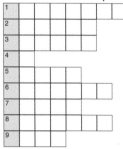

Clues   **1** Maria, ti sento ....! Richiamo. **2** a season   **3** Te lo passo .... (immediately).   **4** ..... accettano solo contanti. **5** garlic   **6** day of the week   **7** Si controllano olio e ....   **8** Non .... (it doesn't matter).   **9** per l'insalata e per la macchina

3 Ring Marco and inform him you are going to the party too. Follow the prompts below. Marco speaks first. *(Answers on page 131.)*

1. Say 'This is ...' and ask 'How are you?'   **2.** Ask 'Are you going to the party tonight?'   **3.** Say 'Yes, what time are you going?'   **4.** Say 'Yes, please'.

Tip

mi 'to me', **ti** 'to you', **gli** 'to him'/'to it', **le** 'to her'/'to it'. These pronouns must be used in conjunction with a verb. They are usually placed in front of the verb, but in some cases they can also come after it. This happens with infinitives following **potere, dovere** and **volere**. Note that in these cases the infinitive loses the final **-e**.

Vorrei parlarle. I would like to speak to her.   **Devo telefonarti** I must ring you.

telefonare, which requires a direct object in English, takes an indirect object in Italian.

Mi telefona. He/she rings me.   **Gli telefono.** I ring him.

Direct and indirect forms of pronouns can combine:

gli+lo = glielo (it to him/to her), **gli+la = gliela** (it to him/to her)
ti+lo = te lo (him/it to you), **ti+la = te la** (her/it to you).

These forms have a range of meanings and only some are included here:

Glielo dico. I say it to him/her.
Te lo passo subito. I'll pass him over to you immediately.

Panorama italiano

Telecom Italia
Telephone numbers can be given either as single digits or in groups of two or three digits, depending on the number. To ring Britain from Italy you need to dial 0044 + the area code number without the 0 (0044–161–456799). To ring Italy from Britain you need to dial 0039 + the area code number with 0 (0039–02–845612). You can buy phonecards (*la scheda telefonica*) at various prices. In some bars you can use the bar phone and pay for the 'units' (*gli scatti*) used.

Time matters

Talking in the past

Vocabolario

la riduzione	reduction
già	already
purtroppo	unfortunately
Toscana	Tuscany
fatto (fare)	made
visitato (visitare)	visited
girato (girare)	travelled around
comprato (comprare)	bought
pagato (pagare)	paid
prenotato (prenotare)	booked
parlato (parlare)	spoken
cucinato (cucinare)	cooked
bruciato (bruciare)	burnt
sbagliato (sbagliare)	made a mistake
ricevuto (ricevere)	received
conosciuto (conoscere)	known
visto (vedere)	seen
dovuto (dovere)	had to
dormito (dormire)	slept
chiesto (chiedere)	asked
sentito (sentire)	heard
hai mai sentito?	have you ever heard?

Dialoghi

Jane talks about her past summer holidays with her friend Paolo.

Jane Quest'estate abbiamo visitato la Toscana.
Paolo Bene, e come avete girato la Toscana, in macchina o in treno?
Jane In treno. Abbiamo comprato un biglietto inter-rail ed abbiamo pagato poco perché abbiamo la riduzione per studenti.
Paolo Dove avete dormito?
Jane Abbiamo prenotato per le prime due notti, poi abbiamo chiesto all'agenzia di turismo del luogo. Abbiamo parlato molto in italiano ed abbiamo conosciuto molte persone.

Nicola tells his colleagues about last night's special meal!

Nicola Ieri mia moglie ha cucinato il pollo. Ma purtroppo ha ricevuto una telefonata ed ha bruciato tutto. Così ha dovuto uscire a comprare una pizza per la cena!

Federica is asking her friend Fabio about a doctor.

Federica Hai mai sentito parlare del Dottor Signorelli?
Fabio Sì, è un nome che ho già sentito. Perché?

Marco has got the wrong number!

Marco Pronto, casa Carulli?
Federica No, qui è Sferlazza.
Marco Oh scusi, ho sbagliato numero.

Esercizi

1 Listen to the conversation and answer the questions below in English. (*Answers on page 131.*)

    1 Where did the speaker go for her holidays?
    2 Where was she taken on her first day?
    3 What did she burn?
    4 What did she buy to make up for it?

2 Look at the pictures below and write what this man has already done. (*Answers on page 131.*)

prenotare
comprare
mangiare

A _____   **B** _____   **C** _____

3 Now ring Michela and tell her what you have done today. Listen to the recording and follow the prompts below. She speaks first. (*Answers on page 131.*)

    1. Say 'Hello, Michela. How are you?' **2.** Say 'I studied.' **3.** Say 'Yes, I have passed and I have received a present.' **4.** Say 'My mother has bought me an inter-rail ticket for this summer'.

Tip

In Italian the present perfect tense is used to express:
1. actions in the recent past (I have just done something, e.g. I have just dropped a plate).
2. (especially in northern Italy) actions completed in the past (I did something, e.g. I received an important phone call). The present perfect is a compound tense, i.e. it has an auxiliary verb and a main verb. For many Italian verbs the auxiliary is **avere** (to have) followed by the past participle of the main verb.

Ho parlato con Luca.	I have spoken to Luca.
Ho ricevuto una telefonata.	I have received a phone call.
Ho dormito bene.	I slept well.

Note that the past participle usually ends in **-ato** (for **-are** verbs), **-uto** (for **-ere** verbs) or **-ito** (for **-ire** verbs).
mai ('never') and **già** ('already') are usually inserted between the two parts of the verb:

Hai mai sentito …?	Have you ever heard …?
Ho già sentito.	I have already heard.

Panorama italiano

Public holidays
Public holidays in Italy are: 1 January (**Capodanno**), 6 January (**Epifania**), Easter (**Pasqua**), Easter Monday (**Pasquetta**), 25 April (the Liberation), 1 May (Feast of the Workers), 15 August (**Ferragosto**), 1 November (**Ognissanti**), 8 December (Immaculate Conception), 25 December (**Natale**) and 26 December (**Santo Stefano**). There are also local holidays and you are strongly advised to check these before your departure. For example, Milan celebrates its local Patron Saint on 7 December, Naples on 19 September, etc.

 **Time matters**

How did it go?

Vocabolario

com'è andata la giornata?	how has your day been?
andato, andata (andare)	gone
stato, stata (essere)	been
svegliato, svegliata (svegliarsi)	woken up
preso (prendere)	taken
speso (spendere)	spent
dovuto (dovere)	had to
diviso (dividere)	divided
partito, partita (partire)	left
vestito, vestita (vestirsi)	got dressed
bagnato, bagnata (bagnarsi)	got wet
divertito, divertita (divertirsi)	enjoyed oneself
successo, successa (succedere)	happened
arrivato, arrivata (arrivare)	arrived
piaciuto, piaciuta (piacere)	liked
affittato (affittare)	rented
insomma	in conclusion
scorso	last
fa	ago
uno stato	a condition
la sveglia	alarm (clock)
che corsa!	what a run/rush!
in fretta	in a hurry

 ## Dialoghi

Marcella tells Stefano about her terrible day yesterday.

Stefano Ciao, Marcella, com'è andata ieri?

Marcella È stata una giornata terribile! Ieri sono andata al lavoro in bicicletta. Ho preparato la bicicletta la sera prima, insomma, tutto pronto per la mattina dopo. La mattina mi sono svegliata presto, mi sono vestita, ho preso la bicicletta e sono partita.

Stefano E che cosa ti è successo?

Marcella Cinque minuti dopo, ha cominciato a piovere! Sono arrivata al lavoro in uno stato terribile!

Valerio speaks to Daniela about his holiday last year.

Daniela Dove sei stato in vacanza l'anno scorso?

Valerio Sono andato in Sardegna.

Daniela E ti è piaciuta la Sardegna?

Valerio Molto! Siamo andati in quattro, abbiamo affittato un appartamento sul mare. Non abbiamo speso molto perché abbiamo diviso le spese per quattro e ci siamo divertiti molto.

Esercizi

1   Listen to the two passages and fill the gaps (*Answers on page 131.*) 🎧

A Ieri mi .... tardi perché non .... sentito la .... Ho ....fare tutto in fretta. Non .... colazione, ... uscita di casa, ... preso la macchina e .... andata al .... Sono .... in orario ma che corsa!

B L'anno .... sono .... in Inghilterra per studiare l'........ Ho .... un corso a Cambridge. Mi .... molto. Ho .... molti inglesi, francesi e .... Durante il fine settimana ho .... un po' .... Oxford, sono .... a Edimburgo, ho .... tre giorni a Londra.

2   Match the two halves to make complete sentences. (*Answers on page 131.*)

A	Sono	**1**	mangiato molto bene da Carla.
B	Ho	**2**	stata molto contenta di vederti!
C	L'anno	**3**	sera ho visto un bel film!
D	Ieri	**4**	scorso non sono andato in vacanza.

3   Listen to the recording and answer the questions. Follow the prompts below. Your friend speaks first. (*Answers on pages 131–32.*) 🎧

1. Say 'I went to the swimming pool'.   **2.** Say 'Yes, I have been to Italy once'. **3.** Say 'Yes, I have eaten tiramisù and I liked it very much'.   **4.** Say. 'No, I have not seen Rome'. **5.** Say 'Yes, I have understood it all'.   **6.** Say 'I haven't seen the car keys'.   **7.** Say 'Yes, I read it last year'.

Tip

In Italian reflexive verbs (i.e. ending in **-arsi, -ersi, -irsi**) and verbs indicating movement use the auxiliary **essere** ('to be') to form the present perfect tense:

Sono andato a Roma.	I went to Rome.
Mi sono alzata tardi.	I got up late.
Sei arrivato presto.	You arrived early.

Note that with **essere** the ending of the past participle agrees with the subject:

Maria è andat*a*   *but*   **Marco è andat*o***
noi (Marco e Carlo) siamo arrivat*i*   *but*   **noi (Marta e Anna) siamo arrivat*e***

Panorama italiano

Italian holidays
Ferries for the islands of Sicily, Sardinia and Elba need to be booked months in advance for travel in the holiday season. The preferred holiday destination for Italians is the seaside, followed by the mountains and the countryside. In the last twenty years the number of Italians going on holiday has increased from 26 to 56 per cent.

Health

Health matters

Vocabolario

male	poorly
i sintomi	symptoms
debole	weak
mancare il respiro	to feel breathless
seguente	following
la stanchezza	tiredness
la maglietta	T-shirt
respiri (respirare)	breathe in
profondamente	deeply
la pressione	blood pressure
le vitamine	vitamins
per sicurezza	for safety's sake
l'esame	test
sentirsi	to feel
svenire	to faint
il lettino	surgery couch
provare	to test
si sieda (sedersi)	sit down
si sdrai (sdraiarsi)	lie down
tossisca (tossire)	cough
mangiare	to eat

Dialogo

Mrs Del Pedro explains to the doctor how she has been feeling during the past three days.

Mrs Del Pedro Buongiorno, dottore. Tre giorni fa, al supermercato mi sono sentita male.

Doctor Che cosa ha sentito? Mi può descrivere i sintomi?

Mrs Del Pedo Sì, mi è girata la testa, mi sono sentita molto debole e mi è mancato il respiro.

Doctor I sintomi sono continuati anche i giorni seguenti?

Mrs Del Pedro La stanchezza sì, e ho sempre mal di testa.

Two minutes later during the examination.

Doctor Allora alzi la maglietta, per favore. Respiri profondamente! Respiri ancora. Benissimo! Adesso Le provo la pressione!

Mrs Del Pedro È qualcosa di grave?

Doctor No, è stanchezza e probabilmente mancanza di vitamine. Per sicurezza Le faccio fare un esame del sangue.

Esercizi

1 Listen to the doctor giving instructions to a patient and match them with the pictures. *(Answers on page 132.)*

A Alzi la maglietta   **B** Tossisca forte   **C** Si sieda   **D** Si sdrai sul lettino

1   **2**   **3**   **4**

2   Match the two halves to make four complete sentences. (*Answers on page 132.*)

   A Mi sono
   B Ho avuto
   C È da tre giorni che
   D Le consiglio

   1 di non mangiare per 24 ore.
   2 mal di stomaco per tre giorni.
   3 non mangio.
   4 sentita male.

3   Now it is your turn to describe your symptoms to the doctor. Listen to the recording and follow the prompts below. You speak first. (*Answers on page 132.*)

   1. Say 'Yesterday I had a headache'.   **2.** Say '39'.

Tip

respiri 'breath in', **si sdrai** 'lie down', **tossisca** 'cough' are forms of command or instruction (formal *Lei*). For all regular **-are** verbs the ending of formal commands is **-i**; for **-ere** and **-ire** verbs the ending is **-a**.

scusi   excuse me!   **prenda!**   take!   **senta!**   listen

There are various ways of expressing a past time. **fa** means 'ago' and is put after the time word: **due giorni fa** ('two days ago'). **scorso** means 'last' and generally goes after the time word preceded by the article **il, la,** etc.: **il mese scorso** ('last month'), **la settimana scorsa** ('last week').

Panorama italiano

Il sistema sanitario italiano
The National Health System (SSN = Servizio Sanitario Nazionale) is free or almost free to everybody. You need to register at your local ASL (Azienda Sanitaria Locale) to obtain a personal card giving you the right for free visits to your GP. A standard fee, known as 'il ticket', is required for medication and tests.

Information

More about telephone conversations and leaving messages

Vocabolario

potrei?	Could I?
impegnato	engaged
la linea	line
lasciare	to leave
lasciar detto qualcosa	to take a message
lasciare un messaggio	to leave a message
dica (dire)	say
che	that
cerco (cercare)	I am looking for
resti (restare)	stay, keep
resti in linea	hold the line
caduto, caduta (cadere)	gone dead
la segreteria telefonica	answering machine
momentaneamente	temporarily
assente	absent
il segnale acustico	beep
venire a prendere ...	to pick ... up
fuori sede	out of the office
incontrare	to meet
passo (passare)	I'm putting (you, etc.) through
come	as in

Dialoghi

Barbara is trying to contact Giovanni.

Barbara	Pronto, potrei parlare con il dottor Giovanni Colucci?
Receptionist	Mi dispiace, ma il dottor Colucci è impegnato sull'altra linea. Devo lasciare detto qualcosa?
Barbara	Sì, per favore, dica che ha chiamato Barbara De Lunghi.

Lucia tries to contact Paolo at the Hotel Raffaello.

Lucia	Pronto, cerco l'ingegner Paolo Morosini, per favore.
Receptionist	Mi dispiace ma non è ancora arrivato. Vuole lasciare un messaggio?
Lucia	Sì, grazie ...

Lucia calls later on.

Lucia	È arrivato l'ingegner Morosini?
Receptionist	Sì, resti in linea, prego ...
Portiere	Scusi, ma è caduta la linea. Attenda che riprovo!

Giovanni leaves a message on Lucia's answering machine.

Segreteria telefonica	Risponde la segreteria telefonica del numero 4–7–6–7–9–0. Siamo momentaneamente assenti. Se volete lasciare un messaggio, fatelo dopo il segnale acustico ...
Giovanni	Ciao, Lucia! Sono Giovanni. Ti telefono per dirti che arrivo domani con il volo AZ 475 delle 9 e 45. Puoi venire a prendermi all'aeroporto? Mi trovi a questo numero di Londra 0181–7–6–5–4–3–2–1 fino a domani alle tre. Ciao.

Esercizi

1 Listen to two messages left on the answering machine and complete the grid in English. (*Answers on page 132.*)

name of caller	telephone number	reason for the call
1		
2		

2 Which is the odd-one-out? (*Answers on page 132.*)

A | lasciare un messaggio | lasciar detto | lasciare Parigi | dica che ho chiamato |

B | la segreteria | rispondere | venire a prendere | il segnale |

C | riprovo più tardi | richiamo | ti telefono! | non importa |

D | il gettone | la scheda | il conto | la cabina telefonica |

3 Leave the message below on Paolo's answerphone in Italian. Prepare it well first, then record it. Once you have recorded it, listen to the model answer which follows. (*Answers on page 132.*)

Say your name (Roberto Spinelli) and spell your surname using the names of Italian towns for each letter. Give your telephone number (06-5-6-7-8-1-2). You are in Rome for two days and would like to meet him. Ask him to ring you back tonight or tomorrow morning.

Tip

non ... ancora means 'not yet'. The adverb **ancora** follows immediately after the auxiliary verb (**essere** or **avere**) in compound tenses . The same rule applies to the majority of adverbs such as **già** ('already'), **appena** ('just') etc:

Ho già mangiato. I have already eaten. **È appena arrivata**. She has just arrived.

Note again the position of **mi, ti**, etc. They usually go in front of the verb, but with infinitives they are added to the end of the verb after dropping the final **-e**:

Vieni a prendermi.   Come and pick me up.
Ti telefono per dirti che ...   I am ringing to let you know that ...

Panorama italiano

Italians use the names of well known cities to spell out words on the telephone. Different people use different cities for the same letter. Mobile phones are very popular in Italy. Having a **cellulare** ('mobile phone') as well as an 'organiser' is part of the concept of **bella figura** ('appearing at one's best') which is deeply embedded in Italian culture.

Health

At the hospital

Vocabolario

fare male	to hurt
gonfio, gonfia	swollen
stia fermo/ferma	keep still
i raggi	x-rays
spiacente	sorry
il gesso	plaster
stare a riposo	to rest
scivolare	to slip
sbattere, battere	to bang
per me	in my opinion
la radiografia	x-ray
nulla di rotto	nothing broken
non si sa mai	one never knows
proprio	really
la roccia	rock
la botta	bruise, blow
la caviglia	ankle
mentre	while
vediamo un po'	let's see

Dialoghi

Mr Mason was skiing and fell. The next day he discovered that his leg had swollen and it was very painful. He therefore decided to go to the hospital.

Dottore	Che cosa si è fatto?
Mr Mason	Sono caduto mentre sciavo e adesso mi fa molto male la gamba.
Dottore	Mi sembra gonfia. Stia fermo per favore! Devo farLe i raggi.

After a while.

Dottore	Sono spiacente, ma devo metterLe il gesso. Deve stare a riposo per un paio di settimane.

Mrs Mangiagalli's little boy fell while playing on the beach. Two days later his face was all bruised and swollen and he could hardly see.

Dottore	Che cosa ha fatto il bambino?
Signora Mangiagalli	È scivolato sulla spiaggia e ha sbattuto il viso su una roccia.
Dottore	Vediamo un po'. Metta questa crema tre volte al giorno e per sicurezza facciamo una radiografia. Per me non c'è nulla di rotto ma non si sa mai.

Esercizi

1   Listen to three medical diagnoses and match them with the appropriate picture opposite. (*Answers on page 132.*)

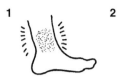   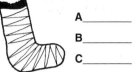

A_____
B_____
C_____

2 Complete the crossword and in the shaded column you will find another important word in case of emergency. (*Answers on page 132.*)

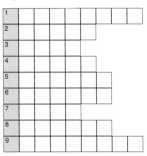

Clues **1** to rent (a flat) **2** while ... **3** a bruise, a blow **4** opposite of **entrata** **5** the couch in a doctor's surgery **6** absent **7** the opposite of **giorno** **8** mosquito **9** to listen to

3 Now it is your turn to explain what happened. Follow the prompts below. The doctor speaks first. (*Answers on page 132.*)

1. Say 'I fell in the kitchen and broke my ankle'. **2.** Say 'Yes, it hurts a lot.'

Tip

Note how **nulla, niente** ('nothing') and **qualcosa** ('something') are followed by **di** if they are accompanied by an adjective:

niente di rotto nothing broken **qualcosa di buono** something good.

Verbs are always in the infinitive when they follow a preposition. In this case the Italian infinitive renders the English '-ing' form:

prima di mangiare before eating **senza dormire** without sleep(ing).

Panorama italiano

The Italian emergency number is 113 for both police and ambulance. When you go abroad on holiday, remember to take your E111 form. It will cover any medical costs and you will receive the same treatment as if you were in a UK hospital. In some cases you may be asked to pay in advance and you will have to claim the money back. It is a good idea to take out insurance if you go skiing.

60 Health

Greetings for any situation

Vocabolario

auguri	wishes
tanti	many
il regalino	small present
l'impegno	commitment
complimenti	congratulations
la promozione	promotion
la bocca	mouth
il lupo	wolf
in bocca al lupo!	good luck! (*literally* 'in the wolf's mouth')
buona fortuna	good luck
cari	dear
cordiale	sincere
sinceri	sincere
distinti saluti	yours sincerely
Natale	Christmas
la guarigione	recovery
crepi il lupo!	may the wolf die!
l'esame	exam

Dialoghi

Eugenio rings Elisabetta on her birthday.

Eugenio	Pronto, Elisabetta?
Elisabetta	Sì, sono io.
Eugenio	Auguri!!! Tanti auguri a te, tanti auguri a te, tanti auguri a Elisabetta, tanti auguri a te!
Elisabetta	Grazie, Eugenio. Ti sei ricordato!
Eugenio	Sì, ho anche un regalino. Quando posso passare?
Elisabetta	Anche subito se vuoi! Non ho impegni!

Marta congratulates Riccardo on his promotion at work.

Marta	Complimenti per la promozione. Sei contento, Riccardo?
Riccardo	Sì, dopo tutto questo tempo!

Carla sends greetings on behalf of Giovanni.

Carla	Monica, ti mando i saluti da parte di Giovanni. Oggi purtroppo non può venire! Ha un esame.

Armando has an exam tomorrow and his university mate wishes him good luck.

Monica	Armando, in bocca al lupo per l'esame di domani!
Armando	Grazie. Crepi il lupo!

Esercizi

1   Your friend Enrico has passed his exam. Which card would you choose for him?
    (*Answers on page 132.*)

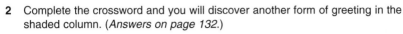

2 Complete the crossword and you will discover another form of greeting in the shaded column. (*Answers on page 132.*)

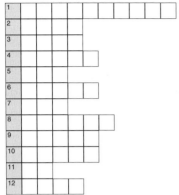

Clues **1** 'congratulations' **2** 'olives' **3** La mamma della mamma di mio figlio è la … **4** contrario di 'forte' **5** un film italiano di Fellini: '… e mezzo' **6** '…' 'Prego!' **7** in bocca al … **8** Vieni anche subito. Non ho … (commitments). **9** Tanti … a te! **10** Buon … e Felice Anno Nuovo! **11** La sorella di tua madre è tua … **12** Fa gli auguri a Monica, deve dare un …

3 Give an appropriate wish for the three situations below. (*Answers on page 132.*)
   1 Monica has just passed her exam.
   2 Giovanni is 23 today!
   3 Barbara is having an interview tomorrow.

Tip

-ino or **-ina** added to the end of a noun can sometimes be used to define something pretty or small:

un tavolo > **un tavolino** (a small table), **un regalo** > **un regalino** (a small present)

But there are exceptions, so always check:

una pianta means 'a plant' *but* **una piantina** means 'a map'.

Panorama italiano

Italians are not in the habit of writing and sending cards for every occasion. They would rather come and see you and wish you Happy Birthday or Happy Christmas in person, or ring you. So don't be disappointed if you don't get a card at Christmas.
There are formal expressions used to open and close letters. Here are a few ways of closing letters: **distinti saluti** is quite formal and corresponds to 'yours sincerely' or 'yours faithfully'; **cordiali saluti** is slightly less formal; **cari saluti** and **affettuosi saluti** are used for friends and family.

Answers

UNIT 1 1 A3, B1, C4, D2
2 1. buonasera; 2. ciao; 3. Sgorlon; 4. Verdi;
5. ingegner. The word in the shaded column
is: **Salve** 3 1. Buongiorno, signora Barilla;
2. Ciao; 3. Buona sera, ingegner Manin;
4. Buona notte, Marta.
Tip ingegner; professor.

UNIT 2 1 Mi chiamo, piacere; Roberto, mi
chiamo 2 **ciao** because it is a form of
greeting and not a reply to an introduction;
scusi because it is an apology, while the
other two are used in introductions;
lentamente because **prego** is the reply to
grazie; (**lentamente** means slowly)
3 1. Buongiorno; 2. Lentamente, per favore;
3. Molto lieta/lieto, mi chiamo ...
Tip 1. piacere; 2, Felice; 3. ciao; 4. Federica;
5. come; 6. mi chiamo.
Panorama Francesca F; Marta F; Marco M;
Carlo M.

UNIT 3 1 1. Marino, American, New York;
2. Federica Biagiotti, Italian, Florence.
2 A2; B4; C1; D3 3 1B; 2C; 3A 4 1. Mi
chiamo ...; 2. Sì, sono inglese; 3. Sono di ...;
4. Prego.
Panorama 1. Naples; 2. Rome; 3. Florence;
4. Turin; 5. Milan; 6. Venice.

UNIT 4 1 A Paul McPherson, Tiziana
Frausin, Pia Pupini; B Renata Gasperini,
Franco Pupini; C Roberto Baggio; D Laura
Ferrari, Sergio Frausin 3 1. • Lei è
insegnante? • Mi chiamo ... Sono ... 2. • Lei è
calciatore? • Mi chiamo ... Sono ... 3. • Lei è
medico? • Mi chiamo ... Sono ... 4. • Lei è
operaio? • Mi chiamo ... Sono ... 5. • Lei è
operaia? • Mi chiamo ... Sono ... 6. • Lei è
insegnante?

UNIT 5 1 AT; BF; CT; DT; EF 2 1. No, è
studente; 2. No, è studentessa; 3. No, io sono
insegnante, Laura è medico; 4. No, è
segretaria in una ditta. 3 in una scuola; A,
B, E, F; in una ditta: D; in un grande
magazzino: C, G.

UNIT 6 1 A 1; B Mr Gandolfi's mother;
C Mrs Bartoli's husband; D Mariella

2 A Giacomo, father; B Marta, mother;
C Valerio, husband; D Valentina, daughter
Practise your possessives mio marito,
mia moglie, mio padre, mia madre, mio figlio,
mia figlia; suo marito, sua moglie, suo padre,
sua madre, suo figlio, sua figlia.

UNIT 7 1 Daniela has written to: mio marito,
mia figlia, mia madre, mia sorella; Daniela still
has to write to: suo padre, suo fratello, suo figlio
2 Buongiorno, signor Colombo; Si, sono
inglese, sono di Londra; Lavoro in un grande
magazzino; No, sono qui in vacanza. 3 1G,
2F, 3A, 4C, 5B, 6D, 7E, The theatre is **La Scala**.
4 1. No; 2. anche; 3. prego; 4. operaio or
operaia; 5. lavoro; 6. io; The city is **Napoli**
(Naples). 5 A16; B1; C12; D11; E2; F3; G15;
H5; I7; J8; K6; L14; M4; N9; O13; P10.

UNIT 8 1 1. 02 816752; 2. 040 475902
3. 0453 863320 4. 0321 875421 2 sei;
diciotto; otto; quindici; cinque; dodici
3 1. Da tre anni; 2. Da diciotto anni; 3. No,
chiave numero quattordici; 4. No questo è il
cinque sette zero, tre quattro due; prefisso
zero uno quattro sette cinque.

UNIT 9 1 trentacinque; cinquantasei;
centosessantasette; milleduecentotrenta-
quattro; ottantacinque; duecentonovanta-
quattro 2 A6; B3; C5; D2; E4; F1
3 trentasette, ottantanove, novanta, tredici,
cinquantacinque, diciannove.

UNIT 10 1 1B; 2A; 3D; 4C 2 1. Luisa,
Cavallaro, italiana, Aosta, segretaria.
2. Michele, Pirelli, italiano, Bologna, operaio.
3 A Scusi, Lei è Madonna?; B Scusi, Lei è
cinese?; C Scusi, Courmayeur è in Francia?;
D Scusi, questo è il pronto soccorso?;
E Scusi, Lei è qui da sola? 4 1. No, non
sono John Travolta; 2. No, Maria non è a
Londra; 3. No, Cosimo non è in Italia; 4. No,
non sono con un gruppo.

UNIT 11 1 A1; B4; C2; D espresso coffee; E
beer 2 A 1 birra, 1 panino al formaggio; B
1 aranciata; C 1 cappuccino, 1 brioche
3 A Vorrei un panino al formaggio, per
favore; B Vorrei due brioche, per favore;

C Vorrei un cappuccino, per favore; **D** Vorrei una birra, per favore; **E** Vorrei un espresso, per favore.

12 **1** **A** Excuse me, where is the restaurant car?; **B** Excuse me where is the toilet?; **C** Excuse me, where is the train for Naples?; **D** Excuse me, is this first class?; **E** Excuse me, where is the second class?; **F** Excuse me, where is the first-aid post?
2 **A** Scusi, dov'è la carrozza ristorante?; **B** Scusi, dov'è il gabinetto?; **C** Scusi, dov'è il treno per Napoli?; **D** Scusi, questa è la prima classe?; **E** Scusi, dov'è la seconda classe?; **F** Scusi, dov'è il pronto soccorso?
3 **A** Venice, Trieste; 5; no further information. **B** Vienna; 2; Romolo. **C** Turin; 7; no further information. **D** Vicenza, Verona, Padua; 1; 1st class front, 2nd class back. **E** Florence; 8; Intercity, dining car back. **4** (The replies are examples of possible answers) **A** Scusi, dov'è il treno per Firenze? Il treno per Firenze è al binario 4. **B** Scusi, dov'è il ristorante? Il ristorante è al primo binario. **C** Scusi, dov'è il gabinetto? Il gabinetto è al binario 3. **D** Scusi, dov'è la prima classe? La prima classe è in testa. **E** Scusi, dov'è il pronto soccorso? Il pronto soccorso è al binario 4.

13 **1** **A** tre; **B** quattro; **C** sette; **D** due
2 **A** 010 75 43 28; **B** 050 33 74 69; **C** 081 17 85 61; **D** 011 92 70 04 **4** Marco ha tre anni; Gianni ha dieci mesi; Marina ha quattro anni; Vieri ha due anni; Anna ha sei mesi.

14 **1** Mi chiamo Robert McClaren; McClaren; No, sono scozzese; Di Glasgow; Main Street trentacinque; Trentacinque; Ingegnere. **2** Quanti anni ha Sara? Diciassette anni; Quando è il compleanno di Sara? Il dodici marzo.
3 formaggio: brioche, panino, coca cola, aranciata, cappuccino;
treno: in testa, prima classe, binario, pronto soccorso, gabinetti

4
il	la	l'	lo
binario	classe	orario	scontrino
gabinetto	carrozza	indirizzo	studente
cognome	brioche	amica	zero
bambino	coca cola	aranciata	zucchero

tempo foto
ristorante borsetta

5 1I; 2F; 3C; 4G; 5E; 6B; 7D; 8H; 9A; The answer is **pendolino**. **6** **A** scuola; **B** orario; **C** scontrino **7** cappuccini; brioche; aranciate; treni; anni; foto **8** di; un; di; ha; in; mamma; Desidera?; una; costa; resto; Prego; per; al; dov'; in **9** Dov'è la prima classe?; Quanto costa questa borsetta?; Quando è il suo compleanno?

15 **1** A2; B3; C1; D4 **2** **A** Quanto; **B** Dove; **C** Siete; **D** Va, andate **3** **A** Ecco il mio passaporto; **B** Cinque giorni; **C** A Palermo; **D** No, sono da solo.

16 **1** **A** zia; **B** nipote; **C** cugine; **D** sorelle **2** 1D; 2A; 3C; 4B **3** **1.** Passo la Pasqua a casa; **2.** Sì, quest'anno faccio il pranzo di Pasqua; **3.** Sì, per tutti i parenti: per due zii, tre nipoti e cinque cugini.

17 **1** A1; B4; D3; F2; blank clocks: 11.50; 1.10 **2** **A** 12.34 p.m.; **B** 6.28 a.m.; **C** 8.05 a.m.; **D** 8 p.m.; **E** midnight/12 p.m. **3** 1B, 2D, 3A, 4C.

18 **1** 1 × Napoletana, 2 × Margherite, 2 × four cheeses, 1 × spaghetti with pesto sauce **2** **A** Mozzarella cheese, tomatoes, anchovies, olives; **B** Mozzarella cheese, tomatoes, Parmesan, basil; **C** four Italian cheeses; **D** basil, pinenuts, olive oil, garlic, Pecorino cheese **3** **1.** Pronto, Pizzeria Romana?; **2.** Vorrei prenotare un tavolo per venerdì sera; **3.** All'aperto, per favore; **4.** Per quattro; **5.** (your name); **6.** Sì, grazie.

19 **1** La Standa: 8.30–13.30; 15.00–20.30; La Banca da lunedì a sabato 8.30–14.00; dal lunedì al venerdì anche 15.00–16.00 **2** **1.** formaggio; **2.** alle; **3.** ri; **4.** mio; **5.** apre; **6.** chiudono; **7.** il; **8.** anche; The Italian shop is **farmacia**. **3** Aprono alle nove e trenta; Chiudono alle sedici e trenta; Aprono alle nove; Chiudono alle venti; Chiudono alle diciassette, diciassette e trenta. **Tip** dal; dallo; dall', dai; dagli; dalla; dall'; dalle.

20 1 £2690; P 12,63; Y 14,76; FF 310; DM 980 2 A4, B5, C2, D1, E3 3 1. Oggi il marco tedesco è a novecentottanta lire; 2. Oggi il franco francese è a trecento e dieci lire; 3. Sul giornale la sterlina è a duemilaseicento e novanta lire; 4. Lo yen è a quattordici lire virgola settantasei; 5. È a dodici lire virgola sessantatré. **Tip** sul; sullo; sull'; sui; sugli; sulla; sull'; sulle.

21 1 1. un; 2. fratello; 3. franco; 4. il; 5. zia; 6. insieme. The museum is **Uffizi** 2 A Alle nove e quindici; B Sono le undici e mezza; C Alle otto e quarantacinque. 3 A 1. Vorrei cambiare cinquecento sterline; 2. Ecco il passaporto; 3. Quant'è la sterlina oggi?; B 1. Vorrei prenotare un tavolo per quattro; 2. All'aperto; 3. Va bene; C 1. Ecco il mio passaporto; 2. Tre settimane; 3. Ecco la mia valigia. 4 Correct order: **C; E; F; B; D; G; H; A** 5 i, gli, le, le, i, i, le, gli 6 1. ora; 2. ritorna; 3. otto; 4. la; 5. orario; 6. giornale; 7. il; 8. ore; clock watch = orologio 7 1. sorella; 2. fratello; zio; 3. sorella; zia; 4. cugini; 5. nipoti 8 1. Che ore sono?; 2. A che ora ritorna in ufficio?; 3. Dove passi la Pasqua?; 4. Quando chiudono i negozi? 9 sul; da; in; alla; dalle; alle; dal; all'; in 10 1. Alle nove; 2. Alle tredici e trenta; 3. Alle ventuno e trenta.

22 1 1B; 2C; 3A; 4E; 5D 2 A5; B4; C1; D3; E2 3 1. Prenda una birra; 2. Prendi un panino; 3. Prenda un caffè; 4. Prendi un gelato; 5. Prendi un'aranciata.

23 1 A alla stazione B al bar C al castello D alla banca E allo zoo 2 La stazione è di fronte all'aeroporto. Il bar Neri è accanto alla scuola. Il pronto soccorso è accanto al castello. La pizzeria è di fronte allo zoo. La banca è di fronte alla scuola. 3 Pronto, taxi Alabarda; Pronto vorrei un taxi per andare al castello; Il suo indirizzo per favore?; Via Cavour 6, accanto alla scuola …

24 1 1. 30 km; 2. circa 30 litri; 3A. 1,86 m, circa 80 kg; 3B. 1,64m, 52 kg; 4. circa 7 km 2 A4, B3, C1, D2, E5 3 1. Peso cinquantasei chili; 2. Milano dista circa seicento chilometri da Roma; 3. Sono un metro e sessantotto.

25 1 A1; B24; C2; D11; mystery word: la spiaggia (see unit 30) 2 A24; B11; C24; D1; E2; F1 3 1. Scusi per andare alla stazione ferroviaria?; 2. Dov'è la fermata, per favore?; 3. Dove posso comprare un biglietto?; 4. Quanto costa un blocchetto?

26 1 A 400 lire all'etto; B 2000 lire al trancio; C 12.000 lire una pizza intera 2 dà, chilo; biscotti, ha; ho, ancora; al 3 1. Vorrei due chili di pane; 2. Quanto costa/Quant'è la pizza?; 3. Ne vorrei due; 4. Sì. Ha biscotti freschi?; 5. Ne vorrei duecento grammi; 6. Quant'è in tutto? **Extra practice** Ne vorrei tre; Marco ne compra due; Ne prendo uno; Ne ho due.

27 1 A3, B4, C2, D1, E5 2 Monday, **Mediterraneo**, by Salvatores; Tuesday, **Otto passi per morire** (A Kiss before Dying) with Matt Dillon; Wednesday, closed; Thursday, **Four Weddings and a Funeral**, British Film Club, with Hugh Grant, in English; Friday, Festival of science fiction movies; Saturday and Sunday, **Pocahontas**, Walt Disney's film, in the open air. 3 Pronto (name of friend), sono (your name), come va? Bene, grazie. Sei libero/libera stasera? Senti, andiamo in una pizzeria all'aperto?

28 1 A caldo/sete; B scendere/papà; C aprono/apre 2 A 1½ chilo; B 1,78 metro; 65 chili; C 20 litri; D 40–50 chilometri 3 ha, va, apre, chiude; ristorante, pizzeria, chiusi 4 1. Di fronte al castello; 2. Accanto alla stazione; 3. È lì di fronte, accanto al castello. 5 1e; 2d; 3a; 4b; 5c; 6f; the name of the piazza is **Navona** 6 1. il; 2. la; 3. passo; 4. ottima; 5. sei; 6. tutto; 7. in; 8. ne; 9. ora The film is **Il Postino**. 7 1. Mi dà un chilo di pane?; 2. Quanto costa la pizza?; 3. Prima di salire, bisogna comprare il biglietto dal giornalaio. 8 Hai; ho; prendi; prendo; è; vorrei; vado; è; dista; sei; pesi; dà 9 trancio; partenza; arrivo; pineta; chilometro; biscotti.

29 1 A1; B3; C2; D5; E6; F4 2 A4; B2; C12; D3; E18 3 Gnocchi al pesto e risotto di scampi come primo; scampi alla griglia e melanzane alla parmigiana come secondo e da bere mezzo litro di vino bianco e acqua minerale. Graham orders items 2 and 6. (The dishes on the menu are: **1.** spaghetti with tomato sauce; **2.** potato dumplings with pesto sauce; **3.** rice and scampi; **4.** T-bone steak; **5.** barbecued scampi; **6.** baked aubergine and cheese dish).

UNIT 30

1

14 tickets for adults	54.600
2 season tickets for child	20.000
Two deck-chairs	35.000
One beach umbrella	45.500
	155.100

2 1. Signora Campana and grandson; **2.** Signori Colombo; **3.** Ms Benson; **4.** The Bruces **3 A** Desidero un abbonamento di dieci ingressi. **B** Desidero noleggiare due sedie a sdraio. **C** Desidero noleggiare un ombrellone.

UNIT 31

1 A2; B4; C3; D1 **2 A** i monumenti rinascimentali; **B** il sentiero per Terme; **C** il centro sportivo; **D** i bagni termali **3 1.** Cerchiamo informazioni su questa zona; **2.** Sì, siamo in macchina; **3.** Ha una mappa, per favore?; **4.** Grazie.

UNIT 32

1 in the museum **2** My house is near the station. From the station take the first on the right, the second on the left and after the second set of traffic lights turn to the right. It is not far. About half a kilometre. I live in the building behind the chemist's. **3 1.** Non lo so. Non sono di qui; **2.** Sempre dritto, la prima a sinistra; **3.** No, è proprio qui, dietro la cattedrale.

UNIT 33

1 A headache and sore throat; **B** sore throat and stomach ache; **C** stomach ache **2 A** headaches; **B** three times a day after meals; **C** 1 spoonful; **D** only from 1 year upwards **3 1.** Ha qualcosa per il mal di testa e per il mal di gola?; **2.** Grazie. Quanto ne prendo al giorno?; **3.** No, grazie. Quant'è?

UNIT 34

1 1B; 2D; 3A; 4C **2** bel; sole; molto caldo; gradi; sereno; nuvola; calmo; buone **3 1.** Pronto, sono .... Chi parla prego?; **2.** Ciao, Elisabetta, che tempo fa a Venezia?; **3.** E il mare è calmo?; **4.** E le previsioni per domani?

UNIT 35

1 1D, 4B, 6C, 5A, 3E, 2F, 7G; **2** 1D, 2C, 3F, 4A, 5G, 6B, 7E **3 1.** Scusi, per andare alla casa di Giulietta?; **2.** Sempre dritto, poi la seconda a destra e in fondo a sinistra; **3.** È lontana da qui? **4 1.** mal di gola; mal di testa; **2.** mal di stomaco **5** da Bruno or Spaghetteria **6 il** bagnino, cugino, cinema, ristorante, secondo, pesce, taxi; **la** sedia, spiaggia, carne, stazione; **lo** zoo, zio, stomaco, sciroppo; **l'**ingresso, ombrellone, amica, ufficio informazioni, albergo **7 io** ho, prendo, vado, vorrei, passo, sono; **tu** sei, prendi, hai, metti; **Lei** ha, dista, consiglia, va, è, desidera, comincia, fa; **noi** andiamo, camminiamo; **voi** desiderate, siete; **loro** fanno, sono **8** A3, B1, C2 **9 A** no; **B** no; **C** yes **10** la prima a destra, poi a sinistra, sempre dritto, poi a destra, la seconda a destra e poi dritto.

UNIT 36

1 quell'ufficio; quello sportello; quel pacco; quella raccomandata; quella bilancia; quelle feste; quegli oggetti; quei francobolli **2 A**2. Non bisogna fumare; **B**5. Non bisogna gettare oggetti; **C**4. Bisogna pesare quel pacco; **D**1. Bisogna spedire quella lettera; **E**3. Bisogna comprare i francobolli. **3 2.** Quel pacco pesa 3 chili; **3.** Quella lettera pesa 20 grammi; **4.** Quella raccomandata pesa 30 grammi; **5.** Quell'armadio pesa 1 quintale.

UNIT 37

1 Correct order: F; D; H; B; G; J; I; A; E; C **2 A** platform 2; **B** platform 1; **C** there is a delay of 12 minutes; **D** first class pre-booked **3 1.** Sì, parlo italiano; **2.** A che ora vuole arrivare? **3.** Allora c'è un solo treno; **4.** Parte da Hull alle sette e trentasei e arriva a Sheffield alle nove e trentatré; **5.** No, è un treno diretto.

UNIT 38

1 benzina; albicocche; pesce **2** un chilo di pomodori, due chili di mele, un

chilo di uva bianca e un chilo di uva nera, tre peperoni, mezzo chilo di fichi, due ciuffi di insalata, un'anguria **3** **1.** Vorrei due chili e mezzo di mele; **2.** Vorrei un chilo di uva; **3.** Bianca, per favore; **4.** Quanto vengono/ costano i peperoni?
Extra practice **1.** capisco; **2** preferisci; **3** preferiscono.

U N I T 39 **1** **A** Gabrio: fair, slim, long straight hair, blue eyes; **B** Martina: small with dark curly hair; **C** Stefano: tall, slim, short dark hair, blue eyes; **D** Luciana: short, plump, fair, straight hair **2** **A**3; **B**1; **C**2; **D**4
3 **1.** Bene, grazie. Quella è la mia amica Luisa; **2.** Quella piccola magra con i capelli bruni e lisci. E li sono i miei amici Stefano e Giorgio; **3.** Quello alto grasso con i capelli ricci è Stefano. **4.** È quello alto magro con i capelli biondi, lunghi e lisci; **5.** Sì, ed è anche molto simpatico.

U N I T 40 **1** 1C giallo; 2E bianco; 3B blu; 4A bianco, rosso, verde; 5D bianco, rosso **2** **1.** verde; **2.** incontrare; **3.** otto; **4.** latte; **5.** arancio   The colour in the shaded column is **viola** **3** **A 1.** Preferisco il rosso; **2.** No, grazie; **B 1.** Cosa mi consiglia?; **2.** Preferisco mangiare piccante; **C 1.** Forte e dolce, prego.

U N I T 41 **1** articolo: gonna; taglia: 42; colore: verde; materiale: pura lana; prezzo: 55.000 lire; la compra/non la compra?: non la compra **2** vorrei, paio, nere, pelle, numero, il; gonna, colore, 50, difficile, taglia, lana, mi, la, camerini, sinistra **3** **1.** Vorrei un paio di scarpe; **2.** nero; **3.** Il trentanove; **4.** Quanto costano?; **5.** Le prendo.

U N I T 42 **1** 1B; 2A; 3C **2** **A:** 7, Bologna; **B:** Mantova, 50 mins late; **C:** 8, Venice; departure 13.20 **3** 1H; 2D; 3B; 4F; 5C; 6G 7J; 8E; 9A; 10I **4** anguria, albicocca, fico **5** 1B, 2C, 3A **6** **A** black and blue, red and black **B** yellow **C** yellow, green, red **7** 1. giallo; **2.** orario; **3.** ritardo; **4.** grasso; **5.** o; 6 nn; **7.** zia; **8.** occhi; **9.** lungo; **10.** anticipo. The name of the cheese is **Gorgonzola**. **8** **A** quante brioche, **B** quante banane, **C** quanti gnocchi, **D** quanti gelati, **E** quanto formaggio, **F** quante olive

9 Mi piace; 1, 3, 6 Mi piacciono: 2, 4, 5 **10** **A** Gianna **B** Marco **C** Gabrio **D** Antonietta **E** Paolo **F** Emanuela **G** Michele **H** Anna ha i capelli corti, ricci e porta la minigonna. È bassa e magra; **I** Leonardo è alto e magro, con i capelli lunghi e biondi. Porta i pantaloni neri e la camicia bianca.

U N I T 43 **1** quello; quello; quello; quelli; quelle; quella **2** lire 900, lire 600, lire 6000, lire 1250, lire 5000, lire 8000, lire 12.000 **3** 1 confezione di yoghurt; 2 confezioni di tortellini; 1 pacchetto di burro; 1 confezione di funghi secchi; 2 etti di pecorino; 1 bottiglia di vino bianco; 1 pacco di pasta.

U N I T 44 **1** A; B; D; F; H **2** prenotare, camera, bagno, pensione, agosto, conferma, parcheggio, telefono **3** **1.** Buongiorno. Vorrei prenotare una camera matrimoniale; **2.** Dal ventitré al trenta maggio; **3.** Quanto costa con la colazione? **4.** Va bene. È lontano dalla spiaggia? **5.** Vorrei prenotare.

U N I T 45 **1** facilities available: 1, 2, 3, 4, 5, 6, 7, 8, 11; not available: 9, 10 **2** **1.** la canadese; **2.** accesso; **3.** tenda; **4.** ore; **5.** rientrare; **6.** cancello; **7.** i campi da tennis; **8.** acqua. The item in the shaded column is: **la torcia** **3** **1.** Avete un posto libero per una tenda per due?; **2.** Per una settimana; **3.** Ecco il mio passaporto. Che attrezzature ha il campeggio?; **4.** È tranquillo di sera?

U N I T 46 **1** B; D; C; A **2** **1.** Riprendo a lavorare alle tre; **2.** di solito guardo la televisione; **3.** qualche volta vado a fare la spesa; **4.** mi vesto; **5.** guardo il telegiornale quando ceno **3** **1.** Mi alzo alle sette; **2.** Esco di casa alle sette e quaranta; **3.** In macchina; **4.** Alle otto; **5.** In ufficio; **6.** Guardo la televisione.

U N I T 47 **1** Nicoletta A; Daniele B **2** **A**3; **B**5; **C**1; **D**2; **E**4 **3** **1.** Mi piace fare sport, mi piace camminare e viaggiare; **2.** Sì, e preferisco la musica classica; **3.** Sì, mi piace andare al cinema e a teatro.

48 1 Paola, good weather: cavalcare; raining: nuoto, ping pong   Marco, summer: pallavolo; winter: sci   2 Massimo + Margherita; Alberto + Valeria; Giorgio + Carla 3 A Massimo piace nuotare, cavalcare e sciare; Giovanna fa il tifo per la Sampdoria, le piace la vela e gioca a pallavolo.

49 1 tre etti di pecorino dolce, un etto di olive nere ed uno di olive verdi, due pacchi di caffè, un chilo di zucchero, tre chili di pasta (spaghetti), due ciuffi di insalata, mezzo chilo di pomodori   2 A Pensione Gardena is best; B Villa Carlotta is too far from the beach; C Hotel Miramare has no garden and you need to cross a road to get to the beach (not suitable for children).   3 Correct order: 3; 4; 6; 2; 1; 5   4 Possible answers: A Il posto tenda è piccolo; B Non c'è un campo da tennis; C I bagni sono lontani; D Non c'è la pineta; E Non c'è acqua calda; F Il minimarket è caro   5 Mariella wakes up at 7.30; gets up at 7.45; has a wash and gets dressed; has breakfast (a brioche bun and a coffee); starts work at 8.30; has lunch from 12.30 till 1.30; goes back home at 5; has her evening meal at 8; sometimes she reads or watches television.   6 Cara Maria, mi sveglio alle …, mi alzo alle …, mi lavo e mi vesto, faccio colazione con una brioche e un caffè, comincio il lavoro alle …, pranzo dalle … alle …, ritorno a casa alle … Ceno alle … qualche volta leggo o guardo la televisione. 7 1 fai; 2 comincia; 3 ascolti; 4 faccio; 5 andate; 6 andiamo; 7 abbiamo; 8 volete; 9 mi alzo; 10 ceni   8 1. scrivere; 2. camminare; 3. Ascolti; 4. colazione; 5. ceno; 6. hotel; 7. incontri   The name in the shaded column is **scacchi** (chess).

50 1 Signora Angelini: 1 June–July; 2 hot water, bathroom, small garden, private beach, sports; 3 quiet, close to sea, clean calm sea; Riccardo: 1 August; 2 self-service restaurant, sailing, tennis, launderette; 3 on the seafront, beautiful scenery   2 1. alle; 2. giocare; 3. roulotte; 4. Italia; 5. tenda; 6. una; 7. R; 8. istruttore; 9. sacco; 10. mi; 11. orario The new word linked with holidays is **agritur-ismo**. ('farm holidays').   3 1. Preferisco il mare; 2. Quest'anno vorrei andare all'estero;

3. In luglio o settembre.   **Grammar practice** 1. so, conosce; 2. so, conosco; 3. sa, conosce.

51 1 Vieri has the largest and Gabrio has the smallest room.   2 A7, B9, C6, D4, E5, F2, F3, G8, H1.

52 1 Correct order: C; D; A; B   2 1. Si fa; 2. bolle; 3. del; 4. si prende; 5. rosolare; 6. d'; 7; si versa   3 1. Ci vogliono circa quindici minuti; 2. Servono un chilo di spaghetti, un po' d'aglio, dell'olio e del peperoncino.

53 1 1A; 2C; 3D; 4B   2 1 accettano; 2 controllano; 3 noleggiano; 4 usano; 5 offre   3 1. Vorrei noleggiare una macchina. Vorrei una macchina italiana. 2. Come si fa per andare all'autostrada per Milano? 3. Quaranta litri di benzina senza piombo, per favore. 4. Può controllare le gomme e l'olio per favore?

54 1 A3; B1; C2   2 1. malissimo; 2. estate; 3. subito; 4. si; 5. aglio; 6. giovedì; 7. gomme; 8. importa; 9. olio   The word in the shaded column is **messaggio**. 3 1. Sono … Come stai?; 2. Vai alla festa stasera?; 3. Sì, a che ora vai?; 4. Sì, grazie.

55 1 1 to England; 2 to a pub; 3 a pizza; 4 wine   2 A Ha già mangiato; B Ha già prenotato la camera; C Ha già comprato il biglietto.   3 1. Ciao, Michela! Come stai?; 2. Ho studiato; 3. Sì, ho passato l'esame e ho ricevuto un regalo!   4 Mia mamma mi ha comprato un biglietto inter-rail per quest'estate.

56 1 A sono alzata, ho, sveglia, dovuto, ho fatto, sono, ho, sono, lavoro, arrivata; B scorso, venuto, inglese, seguito, è piaciuto, conosciuto, brasiliani, visto, della città di, andato, passato   2 A2; B1; C4; D3   3 1. Sono andata in piscina; 2. Sì, sono stata in Italia una volta; 3. Sì, ho mangiato il tiramisù e mi è piaciuto molto; 4. No, non ho visto Roma; 5. Sì, ho capito tutto; 6. Non ho visto le chiavi della macchina; **7.** Sì, l'ho letto l'anno scorso.

UNIT 57 **1** A1; **B4**; **C2**; **D3** **2** A4; **B2**; **C3**; **D1** **3** **1.** Ieri ho avuto mal di testa; **2.** Trentanove.

UNIT 58 **1** **1.** Michela; no telephone number given; just arrived in Milan, will be at Rome railway station at 16.50. **2.** Dr Caselli; 0332-7-6-4-3-1-1-3, fax 0332-7-6-4-3-1-1-5; to confirm hotel booking for 15 June and fix appointment with Dr Cappello for 3 pm
2 **A lasciare Parigi** to leave Paris; **B venire a prendere** to come and pick up; **C non importa** never mind; **il conto** the bill
3 Model answer: Ciao Paolo. Sono Roberto Spinelli, S come Savona, P come Palermo, I come Imola, N come Napoli, E come Empoli, L come Livorno, L come Livorno, I come

Imola. Il mio numero di telefono è zero sei, cinque, sei, sette, otto, uno, due. Sono a Roma per due giorni e vorrei incontrarti. Mi puoi richiamare stasera o domani mattina?

UNIT 59 **1** A3; **B1**; **C2** **2** **1.** affittare; **2.** mentre; **3.** botta; **4.** uscita; **5.** lettino; **6.** assente; **7.** notte; **8.** zanzara; **9.** ascoltare; The word is **ambulanza**. **3** **1.** Sono caduto in cucina ed ho rotto la caviglia; **2.** Sì, mi fa molto male.

UNIT 60 **1** Complimenti **2** **1.** complimenti; **2.** olive; **3.** nonna; **4.** debole; **5.** otto; **6.** grazie; **7.** lupo; **8.** impegni; **9.** auguri; **10.** Natale; **11.** zia; **12** esame Another form of greeting is **condoglianze** (condolences).
3 **1.** complimenti; **2.** buon compleanno/tanti auguri; **3.** in bocca al lupo.

Grammar Summary

Nouns

Nouns are words that label persons, animals, things, places, processes, ideas. Italian nouns are either masculine or feminine. Nouns ending in **o** are usually masculine, nouns ending in **a** are usually feminine, nouns ending in **e** can be either.

Plural nouns

Nouns can be singular (one) or plural (more than one). As a rule masculine nouns ending in **o** change to **i**, feminine nouns ending in **a** change to **e**, and nouns ending in **e** change to **i**. Foreign nouns, nouns ending in consonants, in accented vowels and the few feminine nouns ending in **o** remain the same.

	singular	plural	singular	plural
masculine	amico	amici	calciatore	calciatori
	caffè	caffè	sport	sport
feminine	segretaria	segretarie	madre	madri
	città	città	foto	foto

Articles

These are the words for 'a' and 'the' that go in front of a noun.

The indefinite article 'a'

Masculine: **un** is used before most nouns, **uno** is used before nouns beginning with **s** + consonant, or with **z, x, gn, ps,** or with **i, j, y** (all pronounced i) + vowel.

Feminine: **una** is used before most nouns, **un'** before nouns beginning with a vowel.

The definite article 'the'

Masculine: **il** (*pl.* **i**) is used before nouns beginning with a consonant; **lo** (*pl.* **gli**) is used before nouns beginning with **s** + consonant or with **z, x, gn, ps,** or with **i, j, y** + vowel; **l'** (*pl.* **gli**) is used before nouns beginning with vowels.

Feminine: **la** is used before most nouns; **l'** is used before nouns beginning with a vowel; the plural is always **le**.

	'a'	singular 'the'	plural 'the'
masculine	un magazzino	il magazzino	i magazzini
	un insegnante	l' insegnante	gli insegnanti
	uno yoghurt	lo yoghurt	gli yoghurt
feminine	una ditta	la ditta	le ditte
	un'amica	l' amica	le amiche

Prepositions

Prepositions are words like 'of', 'to', 'in' and 'on'. They stand in front of a noun and link it to the sentence.

In Italian some prepositions combine with the definite article (the) and form a single word. These prepositions are: **a** (to, at), **di** (of), **da** (from, by), **in** (in) and **su** (on).

This is how they combine:

	il	lo	l'	i	gli	la	l'	le
a	al	allo	all'	ai	agli	alla	all'	alle
di	del	dello	dell'	dei	degli	della	dell'	delle
da	dal	dallo	dall'	dai	dagli	dalla	dall'	dalle
in	nel	nello	nell'	nei	negli	nella	nell'	nelle
su	sul	sullo	sull'	sui	sugli	sulla	sull'	sulle

The combined forms **del, della** etc. can also mean 'some':

Vorrei *dei* **giornali italiani.**	I would like some Italian newspapers.
Desidera *del* **ghiaccio?**	Would you like some ice?

Pronouns

Subject pronouns

These are words like 'I', 'you', 'he', 'she' which can replace nouns:

io	I	*noi*	we
tu	you (*sing. informal*)	*voi*	you (*pl. informal and formal*)
lui/lei	he/ she	*loro*	they
Lei	you (*sing. formal*)	*Loro*	you (*pl. very formal*)

tu and *Lei*

Lei is the singular polite form of 'you' and is used to talk to people you are not well acquainted with. **Loro** is the plural but it is falling out of use and is replaced with **voi.**

Lei è **scozzese?**	Are you (*sing.*) Scottish?
Siete **in macchina?**	Are you (*pl.*) driving?

Direct object pronouns

These are words like 'me', 'it', 'them' which are used to indicate the person or object directly affected by the verb. The forms are:

mi	me	*ci*	us
ti	you (*sing. informal*)	*vi*	you (*pl. informal and formal*)
La	you (*sing. formal, fem. and masc.*)	*Li*	you (*pl. very formal, masc.*)
		Le	you (*pl. very formal, fem.*)
lo	him, it (*masc.*)	*li*	them (*masc.*)
la	her, it (*fem.*)	*le*	them (*fem.*)

Lo **conosco**.	I know him.	*La* **compri?**	Will you buy it (*fem.*)?
Vi **hanno veduti al museo.**	They have seen you at the museum.		

Direct object pronouns normally precede the verb form. When they accompany infinitives they are added to the end of the infinitive after dropping the final **e**:

Sono andata a veder*lo* **ieri.**	I went to see him yesterday.
Vieni a prender*mi* **all'aeroporto.**	Come and pick me up at the airport.

Indirect object pronouns

These indicate who or what the action is directed at. Here are the forms:

mi	to me	*ci*	to us
ti	to you (*sing. informal*)	*vi*	to you (*pl. informal and formal*)
gli	to him, to it	*gli*	to them (*pl. colloquial,*
le	to her, to it		*masc. and fem.*)
Le	to you (*sing. formal, masc.*	*loro*	to them
	and fem.)	*Loro*	to you (*pl. very formal,*
			masc. and fem.)

Gli scrivo oggi.	I shall write to him today.
Vi spiegano dove andare.	They explain to you where to go.

Indirect object pronouns normally precede the verb form except for **loro**, **Loro**. When they accompany infinitives indirect object pronouns except for **loro, Loro** are added to the end of the infinitive after dropping the final **e**:

Voglio parlarLe domani.	I want to speak to you tomorrow.

When direct and indirect object pronouns are used together the indirect precedes the direct object pronoun, the *i* in **mi, ti, ci, vi** and reflexive **si** becomes an *e*; **gli, le, Le** become *glie-* and combine with **lo, la, li, le**:

me lo	*me la*	*me li*	*me le*	*ce lo*	*ce la*	*ce li*	*ce le*
te lo	*te la*	*te li*	*te le*	*ve lo*	*ve la*	*ve li*	*ve le*
se lo	*se la*	*se li*	*se le*	*se lo*	*se la*	*se li*	*se le*
glielo	*gliela*	*glieli*	*gliele*	*glielo*	*gliela*	*glieli*	*gliele*

Verbs

Verbs are words that describe actions, feelings or states. The ends of verbs change according to who is doing the action. In dictionaries verbs are always listed with their infinitives (the 'to ...' form of the verb).

Verbs in *-are*, *-ere* or *-ire*

Italian verbs can be divided into three groups according to whether their infinitives end in **-are**, **-ere** or **-ire**. The group in **-are** is the largest, that in **-ire** the smallest. Within these three groups many verbs follow a regular pattern. 'I', 'you' etc. accompany the verb forms only for special emphasis. Here is the present tense.

	abitare (to live)	**chiudere** (to close)	**aprire** (to open)
(io)	abit**o**	chiud**o**	apr**o**
(tu)	abit**i**	chiud**i**	apr**i**
(lui/lei/Lei)	abit**a**	chiud**e**	apr**e**
(noi)	abit**iamo**	chiud**iamo**	apr**iamo**
(voi)	abit**ate**	chiud**ete**	apr**ite**
(loro/Loro)	abit**ano**	chiud**ono**	apr**ono**

Verbs in -*isc*

Many third conjugation verbs (-*ire*) have the following pattern:

capire (to understand) cap**isco**, cap**isci**, cap**isce**, cap**iamo**, cap**ite**, cap**iscono**

Some common verbs in this group are: ***costruire*** (to build), ***finire*** (to finish), ***preferire*** (to prefer), ***pulire*** (to clean)

Common irregular verbs

andare (to go)	**dare** (to give)	**fare** (to do)	**stare** (to stay)	**venire** (to come)
vado	*do*	*faccio*	*sto*	*vengo*
vai	*dai*	*fai*	*stai*	*vieni*
va	*dà*	*fa*	*sta*	*viene*
andiamo	*diamo*	*facciamo*	*stiamo*	*veniamo*
andate	*date*	*fate*	*state*	*venite*
vanno	*danno*	*fanno*	*stanno*	*vengono*

Piacere

Piacere 'to like' is constructed like 'to be pleasing to' in English:

I like science fiction. = science fiction is pleasing to me = ***Mi piace la fantascienza.***
We like olives. = olives are pleasing to us = ***Ci piacciono le olive.***

If a noun indicates who is pleased, this noun is preceded by the preposition **a**:

| **A Vieri piace la pizza.** | Vieri likes pizza. |
| **Al cavallo piacciono le mele.** | The horse likes apples. |

Essere and *avere*

The most important irregular verbs are **essere** (to be) and **avere** (to have), which are known as *auxiliary* verbs. They are used with a form of the main verb called the *past participle* to form a range of tenses. Here are the forms of the present tense:

	essere		**avere**	
(io)	*sono*	I am	*ho*	I have
(tu)	*sei*	you are	*hai*	you have
(lui/lei/Lei)	*è*	he/she/it is	*ha*	he/she/it has
		you are (*sing. formal*)		you have (*sing. formal*)
(noi)	*siamo*	we are	*abbiamo*	we have
(voi)	*siete*	you are (*pl.*)	*avete*	you have (*pl.*)
(loro/Loro)	*sono*	they are	*hanno*	they have
		you are (*pl. formal*)		you have (*pl. formal*)

Modal verbs: *potere, dovere, volere*

These verbs express ability, necessity, probability, wish. They add meaning to another verb in the sentence and are followed by the infinitive. Modal verbs take ***avere*** as their auxiliary.

| **lavoro** I work | ***devo* lavorare** | I have to work | ***ho dovuto* lavorare** | I had to work |
| **dormo** I sleep | ***posso* dormire** | I can sleep | ***ho potuto* dormire** | I was able to sleep |

Here are some useful forms of the modal verbs:

I must	I am able/I can	I want	I should	I could	I would like
devo	*posso*	*voglio*	*dovrei*	*potrei*	*vorrei*
devi	*puoi*	*vuoi*	*dovresti*	*potresti*	*vorresti*
deve	*può*	*vuole*	*dovrebbe*	*potrebbe*	*vorrebbe*
dobbiamo	*possiamo*	*vogliamo*	*dovremmo*	*potremmo*	*vorremmo*
dovete	*potete*	*volete*	*dovreste*	*potreste*	*vorreste*
devono	*possono*	*vogliono*	*dovrebbero*	*potrebbero*	*vorrebbero*

Reflexive verbs

These verbs are called reflexive because in many cases they 'reflect' the action back on the subject as in the sentence 'I wash myself'. They are always accompanied by the reflexive pronouns:

mi myself	*ci* ourselves
ti yourself	*vi* yourselves
si himself, herself, oneself, yourself	*si* themselves, yourselves

The forms of the verb *lavarsi* to wash oneself thus are: **mi lavo, ti lavi, si lava, ci laviamo, vi lavate, si lavano.**

Tenses

The past tense (present perfect)

The present perfect is used to describe something that has happened in the recent past. It is formed with the present of **avere** (to have, used for most verbs) or **essere** (to be) and the past participle of a main verb. Past participles usually end in **-ato** (for **-are** verbs), **-uto** (for **-ere** verbs) or **-ito** (for **-ire** verbs).

ho comprato	I (have) bought	*ho ricevuto*	I (have) received
ho dormito	I (have) slept	*ho capito*	I (have) understood
sono andato	I went/ have gone	*sono caduto*	I fell/have fallen
sono dimagrito	I (have) slimmed	*sono partito*	I (have) left

The past participle of **avere** is *avuto* and that of **essere** is *stato*:

ho avuto	I (have) had	*sono stato*	I was, I have been

The future tense

You can talk about the future by using the present tense and a time expression:

Stasera andiamo al cinema.	Tonight we are going to the cinema.

Giving orders, making requests

Each verb has five endings for the command forms corresponding to **tu**, **Lei**, **noi**, **voi**, **Loro**:

lavora	*chiudi*	*apri*
lavori	*chiuda*	*apra*
lavoriamo	*chiudiamo*	*apriamo*
lavorate	*chiudete*	*aprite*
lavorino	*chiudano*	*aprano*

Adjectives

Adjectives describe nouns. Adjectives in Italian take the same gender (masculine/feminine) and number (singular/plural) as the nouns they describe. Adjectives normally follow the noun. Adjectives of nationality are written with a small letter.

Adjectives ending in -o

These have four forms:

il ragazzo *italiano*	i ragazzi *italiani*
la ragazza *italiana*	le ragazze *italiane*

Adjectives in **-co** and **-go** add an **h** before the plural ending to keep the sound:

un film *lungo*	a long film	**due libri *lunghi***	two long books
un clima *secco*	a dry climate	**i funghi *secchi***	dried mushrooms

Adjectives ending in -e

These adjectives have two endings: one for the singular and one for the plural:

il libro *inglese*	i libri *inglesi*
la signora *inglese*	le signore *inglesi*

un museo *interessante* an interesting museum	**l'acqua *minerale*** mineral water

buono and *bello*

When **buono** (good) and **bello** (beautiful) are used before the noun they take endings similar to those of the article **un** and of the article **il** respectively. Here are some examples:

buon viaggio	***buono*** studente	***buona*** brioche	***buon'*** idea
bel tempo	***bello*** spettacolo	***bella*** piazza	***bell'*** ambiente
bei giardini	***begli*** scampi	***begli*** amici	***belle*** vacanze

questo and *quello*

questo (this) follows the same pattern as adjectives in **-o**. The forms of the adjective ('this', 'these' before a noun) and those of the pronoun are the same:

questo formaggio	desidero ***questo***	***questa*** ricotta	preferisco ***questa***
queste olive	vorrei ***queste***	***questi*** tortellini	mangiamo ***questi***

The adjective **quello** (that) goes before the noun and takes forms similar to those of **il** and **bello**. Here are some examples:

quel carrello	***quello*** zucchero	***quell'*** albergo	***quella*** valigia	***quell'*** agenzia
quei pannolini	***quegli*** antipasti	***quegli*** studenti	***quelle*** gonne	***quelle*** idee

quello (that) has the following regular forms when it is a pronoun:

singular	***quello***	***quella***	plural	***quelli***	***quelle***

Making comparisons

Più (more) and **meno** (less) are used in front of adjectives to compare people and things. To say *than* use **di** in front of nouns, pronouns and numbers and **che** in all other cases.

Questa stanza è *meno* **bella** *di* **quella.**	This room is less nice than that one.
Matteo è *più* **alto** *di* **Gabrio.**	Matthew is taller than Gabrio.
Il mio giardino è *più* **lungo** *che* **largo.**	My garden is longer than wide.

Possessive adjectives and pronouns

The forms of the possessive adjectives and pronouns are identical. Like all other adjectives possessive adjectives take the gender (masculine/feminine) and number (singular/plural) of the noun they accompany, in this they are different from English.

Possessive adjectives have four forms except for **loro** (their/theirs) which is invariable. Possessives are placed before the noun they accompany and are normally accompanied by the definite article. The article is however omitted with all possessives except **loro** when describing one family relation: *mio* **padre**, *tua* **madre**, *sua* **zia**, *nostro* **cugino**, *vostro* **fratello**, *la loro* **nonna**.

Here are the forms:

il mio	*la mia*	*i miei*	*le mie*	my, mine
il tuo	*la tua*	*i tuoi*	*le tue*	your, yours (*sing. informal*)
il suo	*la sua*	*i suoi*	*le sue*	his, her, hers, its
il Suo	*la Sua*	*i Suoi*	*le Sue*	formal your, yours (*sing. formal*)
il nostro	*la nostra*	*i nostri*	*le nostre*	our, ours
il vostro	*la vostra*	*i vostri*	*le vostre*	your, yours (*pl. informal and formal*),
il Loro	*la Loro*	*i Loro*	*le Loro*	their, theirs
il Loro	*la Loro*	*i Loro*	*le Loro*	your, yours (*pl. formal*)

il mio conto	my bill	*la mia ditta*	my firm	*i miei libri*	my books
i tuoi amici	your friends	*le tue sorelle*	your sisters	*la loro* **automobile**	their car

Questions

The word order in questions is the same as in statements. To find out more a question word can be added at the beginning of the question:

Quando **andiamo in piscina?** When are we going to the swimming pool?

Here are some useful question words:

chi? who?	*dove?* where?	*quando?* when?	*come?* how?
che cosa?/cosa? what?		*quanto/a* how much?	*quanti/e* how many?

Vocabulary

This list contains some of the most important Italian words from the course. Translations and forms have been reported as they appear in the dialogues or/and exercises. In many cases, other meanings are possible. Please refer to a dictionary for more detailed information.

Nouns: The gender is indicated for nouns through their definite article (il, la, lo, l') placed after the word. The plural of irregular nouns is provided (e.g. albicocca, *pl.* albicocche). If a noun can be used only in the singular or plural form, it is stated (e.g. uva *sing.*; capelli *pl.*).
Verbs are given in the infinitive form only; in some cases, the irregular form of the past participle will be indicated (e.g. prendere – *pp.* preso); if reflexive it will be indicated. If irregular in many forms, it will be stated by the abbreviation '*irreg.*'
Adjectives are given in their masculine singular form. In some cases this is followed by the feminine form. The plural is provided only if irregular (e.g. bianco/a; *pl.* bianchi/bianche).
List of abbreviations: *adj.* adjective; *invar.* invariable; *irreg.* irregular verb; *reflex.* reflexive verb; *pp.* past participle of verb; *pl.* plural; *sing.* singular.

A

abbonamento (l'; gli)   season ticket
abitare   to live
accanto a   next to
accesso (l'; gli)   access
adesso   now
adorare   to love, to be mad about
affittare   to rent
aggiungere   to add
aglio (l')   garlic
albergo (l'; gli alberghi)   hotel
albicocca (l'; le albicocche)   apricot
allora   then
alto *adj.*   tall
altro *adj. & pronoun*   other
alzarsi *reflex.*   to get up
amaro *adj.*   bitter
ambiente (l'; gli)   environment
(l') amico/a (gli amici/le amiche)
   friend (friends)
anche   also
ancora   still, again
andata (l')   single ticket
anguria (l')   water melon
anticamera (l')   hall
(in) anticipo   early, in advance
aperto *adj./*all'aperto**   open/outdoors
apertura (l')   opening
appena   just
aprire (*pp.* aperto)   to open
aranciata (l')   orange squash
arancio *adj. invar.*   orange
arena (l')   open-air theatre
arrivo (l'; gli)/in arrivo   arrival/on its
   way
ascoltare   to listen to
(per) asporto   to take away
assaggiare   to taste
attrezzature (le) *pl.*   facilities
auguri (gli) *pl.*   wishes
autostrada (l')   motorway
avanti!   come in

B

bagagliaio (il; i bagagliai)   boot
bagnarsi *reflex.*   to get wet
bagnino (il; i)   beach attendant
bagno (il; i)   bathroom
bandiera (la)   flag

basta   enough
bel/bello/bella *adj. irreg.*   beautiful
benzina (la)   petrol
bianco/a (bianchi/bianche) *adj.*   white
bilancia (la)   scales
binario (il; i)   platform
bisogna   it is necessary, one has to
(aver) bisogno di...   to need
bivio (il)   junction
bocca (la; le bocche)   mouth (mouths)
bocce (le) *pl.*   bowls
borsetta (la)   handbag
bosco (il; i boschi)   wood (woods)
botta (la)   bruise
bruciare   to burn
bruno *adj.*   dark-haired
brutto *adj.*   bad
buon, buono, buona *adj.*   good

C

cabina telefonica (la)   telephone box
cadere   to fall down, to go dead
   (telephone line)
calcio (il) *sing.*   football
caldo *adj.*   hot
cambiare   to change
cambio (il; i)   exchange rate
camera (la)   room
camera da letto (la)   bedroom
camerino (il; i)   changing room
camicetta (la)   blouse
camminare   to walk
canadese (la)   tent for two
cancello (il)   gate
cantante (il/la)   singer (male & female)
capelli (i) *only pl.*   hair
capire *irreg.*   to understand
carne (la)   meat
caro *adj.*   expensive, dear
carrello (il; i)   trolley
carrozza (la)   carriage
carrozza ristorante (la)   dining car
casa (la)/a casa   home, house/at
   home
casello (il; i)   tollgate
cassetta (la)   crate
cavalcare   to ride
cavallo (il; i)   horse

caviglia (la; le caviglie) ankle
cenare to have dinner
cercare to look for
che what, that, which
chi who
chiamare to call
chiave (la) key
chiedere (*pp.* chiesto) to ask
chiudere (*pp* chiuso) to close
chiusura (la) closing
cielo (il; i) sky
ciliegia (la; le ciliege) cherry
cilindrata (la) engine size (*lit.* cubic capacity)
ciuffo (il; i) head (of salad)
(in) coda at the rear
cognome (il) surname
coincidenza (la) connection
colazione (la) breakfast
colpo (il; i) blow, strike
commesso/a (il/la) salesman/woman, shop assistant
commissariato (di polizia) police station
compleanno (il; i) birthday
comprare to buy
confezione (la) pack
conoscere to know
cordiale *adj.* warm
corridoio (il; i) passage
corto *adj.* short
cucchiaio (il; i cucchiai) spoon spoonful
cucina (la) kitchen
cucinare to cook
cuocere *irreg.* to cook

D dare *irreg.* to give, to show (of films)
data (la) date
debole *adj.* weak
destra (la) right
(a) destra/sulla destra to the right/on the right
di solito usually
dire (*pp.* detto) *irreg.* to say/to tell
dispiacere to be sorry
disponibile *adj.* available, helpful
distare to be far
distinti saluti yours sincerely
disturbato *adj.* bad (telephone connection)
ditta (la) firm
divertirsi *reflex.* to enjoy oneself
dividere (*pp.* diviso) to divide
doccia (la; le docce) shower
dolce *adj.* mild, sweet
dopo after, later
dormire to sleep
dovere to have to
duomo (il; i) main church

E ecco here/there is
(all') estero abroad
etto (l'; gli) 100 grams

F

fa ago
fame (la) *sing.* hunger
fantascienza (la) *sing.* science fiction
fare (*pp.* fatto) *irreg.* to do, to make
colazione to have breakfast
collezione di to collect
il tifo per ... to be a supporter of ... (football team)
la spesa to do the shopping
sport to practise sport
farsi male *irreg. reflex.* to hurt oneself
fegato (il) liver
fermata (dell'autobus) (bus) stop
fermo *adj.* still
figlio/a (il/la) son/daughter
fila (la) queue
fino a up to
flacone (il; i) bottle
(in) fondo a at the end of
formaggio (il; i) cheese
forte *adj.* loud, strong, intense
francobollo (il; i) stamp
fratello (il; i) brother
freddo *adj.* cold, chilled
fresco/a (freschi/fresche) *adj.* fresh
(in) fretta in a hurry
frollino (il; i) shortbread biscuit
fumante *adj.* steaming
fungo (il; i funghi) mushroom
fuori outside

G

gabinetto (il; i) toilet
(in) gamba bright, smart
gesso (il; i) plaster
ghiaccio (il) ice
già already
giallo/a *adj.* yellow
giocare a to play (sport, game)
giornalaio (il; i) newsagent
giornale (il; i) newspaper
girare to travel around
gola (la) throat
gomma (la) tyre
gonfio *adj.* swollen
gonna (la) skirt
granchio (il; i granchi) crab
grasso *adj.* fat
guarigione (la) recovery

I

impegnato *adj.* engaged, busy
impegno (l'; gli) commitment
incontrare to meet
incrocio (l'; gli incroci) crossroads
ingresso (l'; gli) admission ticket
inoltre as well
insegnante (l'; gli/le) teacher (male or female)
insieme together
insomma in conclusion
interno (l'; gli) flat number, extension number
invece instead

lasciar detto qualcosa to leave a message **L**

lasciare to leave
lavanderia a gettoni launderette
lavarsi *reflex.* to get washed
lavorare to work
lavoro (il) work
leggere (*pp.*** letto)** to read
lettino (il; i) surgery couch
lì there
libro (il; i) book
lieto/a *adj.* **; molto lieto** glad; how do you do
liscio *adj.* straight
lungo/a (lunghi/lunghe) *adj.* long

M **ma** but
madre (la) mother
maglietta (la) T-shirt
mal di... + *sing. noun* ... ache
mal di testa headache
mancare il respiro to feel breathless
mansarda (la) converted attic
marito (il; i) husband
marrone *invar.* brown
medico (il; i medici) doctor
mela (la) apple
melanzana (la) aubergine
mentre while
mescolare to stir
mese (il; i) month
mettere (*pp.*** messo)** to put
mezzanotte (la) midnight
mezzogiorno (il) *sing.* midday
miglio (il; le miglia) mile
moglie (la) wife
moneta (la) change, coins
mosso *adj.* rough
movimentato *adj.* busy

N **Natale (il)** Christmas
ne of it/them
negozio (il; i) shop
nero/a *adj.* black
nipote (il/la) nephew/niece
noleggiare to rent, to hire
nome (il; i) first name
nulla nothing
nuotare to swim
nuoto (il) *sing.* swimming
nuvola (la) cloud
nuvoloso *adj.* cloudy

O **occhio (l'; gli)** eye
(in) offerta on special offer
oggi today
ombrellone (l'; gli) beach umbrella
operaio/a (l'; gli/le) factory worker
orario (l'; gli)/in orario timetable/on time

P **padre (il; i)** father
paesaggio (il; i) scenery, landscape
paese (il; i) village
pagare to pay
pallacanestro (la) *sing.* basketball
pallavolo (la) *sing.* volleyball

pane (il) *sing.* bread
panetteria (la) bakery
panino (il; i) roll
pannolino (il; i) nappy
parente (il; i) relative
partenza (la) departure
partire to leave
partita (la) match
Pasqua (la) Easter
passaggio (il; i) lift (as in ask for a lift)
passare to put through, to put on, to come by
passata (la) sieved tomatoes
passeggiata (la) walk
pastiglia (la) tablet
pasto (il; i) meal
patente (la) driving licence
pelle (la) leather
pensare to think
pentola (la) pot
peperoncino (il; i) chilli pepper
peperone (il; i) red pepper
perché because, why
pernottamento (il; i) overnight accommodation
pesare to weigh
pesca (la; le pesche) peach
pesce (il; i pesci) fish
Piacere! How do you do?
piantina (la) map
piccante *adj.* spicy
pieno *adj.* full
pineta (la) pine wood
ping pong (il) table tennis
pioggia (la) rain
piombo (il) lead
piscina (la) swimming pool
poi then
pomodoro (il; i) tomato
posto (il; i) place
(a) posto in order
posto tenda a space for a tent
pranzare to have lunch
pranzo (il; i) lunch
prefisso (il; i) code
prendere (*pp.*** preso)** to take
prenotare to book
prenotazione (la) reservation
previsioni del tempo (le) weather forecast
prima di before
primo/a *adj.* first
pronto *adj.* ready, ready-made
pronto soccorso (il) *sing.* first-aid post
proprio really
provare to try on, to test
pure also
purtroppo unfortunately

Q **qua** here
qualche volta sometimes
qualcosa something
quale? quali? which?
quando? when?
quei, quegli, quelle *adj.* those

quel, quell', quello, quella *adj.* that
questo, questa, questi, queste this, these

R **resto (il)** *sing.* change
riccio *adj.* curly
ricetta (la) recipe, prescription
rimanere (*pp.* rimasto) *irreg.* to stay
ripasso (il; i) revision
riunione (la) meeting
rosa *adj. invar.* pink
rosolare to brown
rosso/a *adj.* red
roulotte (la; le) *invar.* caravan
rucola (la) *sing.* rocket

S **sacco a pelo (il; i sacchi a pelo)**
sleeping bag
sala (la) lounge, dining room
salato *adj.* salty
sale (il) *sing.* salt
salire *irreg.* to get on
salumeria (la) delicatessen
sangue (il) *sing.* blood
sapere *irreg.* to know
saporito *adj.* tasty
sbagliare to make a mistake
sbattere to bang
scala (la) stairs
scarpa (la) shoe
scendere (*pp.* sceso) to get off
sciogliere (*pp.* sciolto) *irreg.* to melt
scivolare to slip
scolare to drain
scontrino (lo; gli) payment slip
scorso *adj.* last
scrivere (*pp.* scritto) to write
sdraiarsi *reflex.* to lie down
secco *adj.* dry
sede (la) headquarters/office
sedersi *reflex.* to sit down
sedia (la); sedia a sdraio chair;
deck-chair
segnale acustico (il; i) beep
segreteria telefonica (la) answering
machine
seguente *adj.* following
seguire to follow
semaforo (il; i) traffic lights
sembrare to look, to seem
sennò if not, otherwise
sentiero (il; i) path
sentire to listen
sentirsi *reflex.* to feel
senza without
serbatoio (il; i) tank
sete (la); aver sete thirst; to be thirsty
settimana (la) week
sinistra (la) left
sole (il) *sing.* sun
sonno (il); avere sonno sleep; to be

sleepy
sorella (la) sister
spendere (*pp.* speso) to spend
spiacente *adj.* sorry
spiaggia (la) beach
sportello (lo; gli) counter
squadra (la) team
stagionale *adj.* season
stanchezza (la) tiredness
stare a riposo to rest
statale national, strada statale 'A' road
studente (lo; gli) student (male)
studentessa (la) student (female)
subito immediately
succedere (*pp.* successo) to happen
suonare to play (instrument)
superare to overtake
sveglia (la) alarm
svegliarsi *reflex.* to wake up
svenire to faint

T **taglia (la)** size (for garments)
telegiornale (il) *sing.* news on TV
tempo (il; i) time,weather
temporale (il; i) storm
terzo *adj.* third
testa (la)/in testa head/at the head
torneo (il; i) competition
traghetto (il; i) ferry
trancio (il; i) slice
tranne (+ il/lo/la etc) except for
troppo too much of it/them
trovare to find
tutto *adj.* all

U **un po'** a bit
unico/a unici/uniche the only one
uscire *irreg.* to go out
uscita (l') exit
uva (l') *sing.* grapes

V **valigia (la; le valigie/valige)** suitcase
vedere (*pp.* visto) to see
vela (la) sailing
venire a prendere to pick ... up
verde *adj.* green
versare to pour
vestirsi *reflex.* to get dressed
vetrina (la) shop-window
via (la) street
via aerea; via mare by air; by sea
viaggiare to travel
volentieri gladly
(una) volta once
volte times

Z **zafferano (lo)** *sing.* saffron
zio/a uncle/aunt
zucchero (lo) *sing.* sugar

Language and Topic Indexes

Numbers refer to units.

Numbers in bold indicate that an irregular verb is reported at the end of the unit and the full form will be in the grammar summary.

LANGUAGE

a
  uses of 25, 29, 37, 53
  with definite articles **(il, la** etc.) 19
adjectives 3, 6, 18, 31, 40
  demonstrative 5
  possessives 6, 39
  invariables 40
  irregular 39, 60
adverbs 56, 58
age 13
andare 23, 25, 27, 48
articles
  definite **(il, la)** 9, 11, 12, 15, 16
  indefinite **(un)** 4, 8
  use of 4, 15, 16
avere
  idioms with **13, 22**
  auxiliary **56**
bello 51
buono 22
c (pronunciation of) 2
c'è, ci sono 20
che 34, 39, 47, 51
chi 34
ci
  idiomatic expressions 37
  with **'ne'** 45
  as reflexive pronoun 46
  as indirect object pronoun 29
comparisons more/less 51
conoscere 50
da
  uses of 19, 30, 41
  with definite article 19
dare 26
dates 44
days of the week 18
di
  uses of 20, 59
  with definite article 20
  as partitive 11, 52
  with comparisons 51
direct object 3
dovere 33
e, ed 3, 17
elision with titles 1; pronouns 33, 54, 58
essere   3, 13, 17
  idioms with **40**

fare 26, 48, 15
  gender 3, 5
imperative forms, see Verbs
in
  with definite articles 25
indirect object 26, 29, 33, 54
la/lo/le/li
  direct/indirect objects 33, 41
Lei 2, 22, 27
mi/me
  direct/indirect object 26, 29, 54
molto 28
months of the year 44
ne 26, 33, 45
non and negatives 10
nouns
  gender of 4
  plural of 12
  invariable 12, 47
  irregular 24
numbers
  (0-19) 8
  (19-2000) 9
  handwritten 12
  ordinal numbers 12
  telephone 8
past participle, see Verbs
per 53
piacere 41
possessive adjectives and pronouns 6, 15
potere 48
prendere 25
prepositions (other than separately listed) 23, 25, 59
present tense indicative, see Verbs
pronouns
  direct and indirect object 3, 26, 29, 33, 41, 54
  subject 4, 8
qualcosa 59
quale 43
quanto 13
quel/quello 36
reflexive verbs, see Verbs
sapere 50
si
  impersonal construction 52
  passive voice with 52, 53
  with reflexive verbs 46
stare
  idioms with 41
su 20
titles 1, 2, 4, 12
tu/Lei 22, 27
tutto 45
un/una, see Articles
venire 38, 48
verbs
  present indicative (**-are**; **-ere**

  -ire) 22, 24, 27, 30, 31, 38
  irregular 48
  reflexives 46
  present perfect of 56
  past participle of 56
  imperative 32, 57
  impersonal form 25
  infinitive 30
volere 37

TOPICS

Accommodation 44, 51
Beach 30
Cafeteria, café, restaurant 11, 12, 18, 22, 29
Camping 45, 50
Days, months 9, 18,44
Describing
  Colours, smells, flavours 40
  Daily routine 46
  People 39
Directions 32
Emergency 59
Family 6, 13, 16
Forms (filling in) 10
Greetings 1, 2, 3, 4, 60
Health 10, 33, 57, 59, 60
Hobbies and pastimes 27, 47, 48
Holidays 50, 55, 56
Hotel 44
Italian cuisine 26, 52
Money and payment 18, 20
Motoring
  Motorways 53
  Petrol station 53
Nationality 3, 10
Numbers 8, 9, 13, 20, 24
Passport 15
Past (talking in the) 55
Post office 36
Regions 3
Shopping
  Clothes 41
  Food 22, 26, 38, 43
  Opening hours 19
Sport 48
Supermarket 43
Telephone 8, 54, 58
Time 13, 17, 56
Tourist office 31
Travel
  Bus and coach 25
  Car (hire) 53
  Plane 15
  Taxi 23
  Train 12, 37
Weather 34
Weights and measurements 24
Work 4, 5, 10